DID IT ON A DARE

DID IT ON A DARE

How I Built a Comedy Empire

in 30 Short Years

By

Al Martin

With Ginger Reiter

ISBN-9798646230035

Cover Design by Drew Tessier

Copy Editor Ian Wehrle

Edited by Ginger Reiter

CONTENTS

PROLOGUE

I am the world's biggest Al Martin fan. Al can open a successful comedy club in ANY location, and I know he will be the first to figure out how to present post-pandemic standup. When I moved to NYC from San Francisco in 1999, Al gave me my first break. He saw me in the "Little Room" at New York Comedy Club (yes, he opened a small comedy club INSIDE his large comedy club) and told me to call in for spots.

I will never forget that night, he made me a New York comic. Al doesn't get enough credit for booking balanced shows. At that time in NYC, it was common for clubs to book no women, or just one woman per show. Al never thought that way. I met some of my favorite women comics when we were booked together on an Al Martin show. Is Al cheap?

Yes. So cheap he should be studied by experts. But he's cheap with everyone, equally. While he was underpaying me, I couldn't complain because he was underpaying all of us. Love you Al, I can't wait to send in my avails to Covid Comedy Club!

Laurie Kilmartin

INTRODUCTION

Al Martin continues to be a comedy muse to some and a thorn in the side to others in the comedy world, but make sure of one thing – he was and still is instrumental in the birth of post modern comedy that began in the nineties. He let me have a one man show every Monday for 2 1/2 years. Most importantly he let me misbehave. He let me try any joke – any style so I could find my comedy voice which thanks to Al became my introduction *"Steve's not politically correct and he's not here to behave."*

Both Al and I are from Brooklyn and that is an important part to understanding him. We both grew up at a time of religious prejudice and danger. We both had the same threatening experience of riding the D train when we were kids. Different cultures control different neighborhoods and simple things like playing schoolyard basketball in someone else's neighborhood was a risk. We were often picked on because of our religion or because we looked different. I believe this motivated Al (in part) to be successful.

I'd like to keep writing but I'm getting "the light" and truthfully I've got to get to Chapter One and begin reading this book. I'm so excited to hear Al's retelling of his life as a comedian, club owner and one of the many Brooklyn boys who made a name for himself.

Steve Marshall

FOREWORD

This book will wake you up like an Ice Bucket Challenge dumped on your head, showing you exactly how to become the person you've dreamed of becoming.

Al Martin is the perfect of example of someone who the comedy business took little notice of because he never made the 'Big Splash'. Instead he pursued his passion until he created 'Tidal Wave'!

If life were a pick up basketball game, the comedy industry would be The Bullies and Al Martin would be the last kid picked. However, as the game went on The Bullies would realize they screwed up. They got schooled and Al would hit the last shot. And *he'd* have next.

If you ever feel you've been overlooked, underestimated, this book will inspire you to wake up and realize the only opinion of you that matters is YOURS.

Enjoy reading The Rise and Rise of one of the most influential Comedy Club owners.

Chris Murphy

DEDICATION

I dedicate this book to my sister Debbie, who I lost during the time of Covid19. She suffered a myriad of illnesses throughout her life but she was the strongest and toughest person I knew. Whenever I would get down on myself Debbie's grit and toughness pulled me through. The world for me will not be the same without her selflessness.I will forever have her in my thoughts.

I also would like to dedicate this book to my beautiful wife Carolyn who I have tortured with hundreds of jokes and creative ideas through the years. Thank God she has great patience and a great set off...earphones.

CHAPTER 1

First Time for the Fat Guy

The year was 1989 and my life was pretty much a train wreck (which I never guessed would qualify me later on to become a stand-up comic). I had gotten married very quickly and just as quickly, was divorced. I had built up several successful businesses which through no fault of my

own would suddenly fail miserably.

One of them was legislated out of business. Believe it or not, I used to do lie detector tests. I was a polygraph examiner, and I had built one of the largest polygraph firms in the entire city of New York. We took up an entire floor. I was continually reinvesting my money to make the business bigger and bigger. Then, in the late 1980s, Senator Ted Kennedy introduced a bill outlawing the use of the polygraph for pre-employment purposes. President Reagan was against it, but, in some good old fashioned horse trading, he acquiesced if Kennedy would sign off on another bill that Reagan wanted. Since there were tens of thousands of citizens that needed Reagan's legislation, and only a couple of thousand polygraph examiners in the entire country, politics prevailed.

I had one year to close my business which was essentially giving polygraph exams to aspiring employees throughout Manhattan. Life was not following the game plan I had set out for myself. I was a rudderless ship, single and broke, with a five year old child to support. It just so happens that I was dating a girl at the time who was a stand-up comedian.

A lot of people "say" they're stand-up comedians. She appeared at open-mics which I knew nothing about. I was different than most people in the comedy business. Talk to people in comedy. They aspire their whole lives to become comedians. That wasn't me. I was geared to become a business person or a lawyer when I was younger. Those were my aspirations – but the law thing just didn't work out. I also had a slight case of attention deficit disorder (well, a little more than a slight case) and I really couldn't focus on the books. This was before Ritalin became chic. Anyway I was encouraged by this girl to watch her do stand–up comedy.

Typically she would do her set, then, as women are apt to do, she'd ask "How was I?" Now, if I've learned one thing in life it's this: when a woman asks, "Do I look skinny?" or "Was I good?" or she asks how anything is, the answer is automatically, "yes" or "great". Otherwise you wind up in a twelve hour debate and your head will be exploding. So my answer is always, "Yes". Was I funny? "Yes!" On and on she asks me the same question; finally I couldn't take it anymore. So I turned to her and I said, "You know what? You really sucked! You weren't that funny. It was horrible to listen to. Does that make you happy"? Well, that led to a fifteen minute argument where we were hurling insults at each other, when she suddenly turned around to me and said: "Oh, so you think you're so funny. I dare you to get on stage."

A week later, I was at an open mic at Pips Comedy Club in Brooklyn, when, after I had waited three hours for my turn, Andrew Dice Clay walks in ready to do a run through for his 1989 HBO special. Well, Dice was up there 45 minutes (it was by now, close to one o'clock in the morning) and he crushed the room.

Everybody ran to the back of the Comedy Club clamoring for his autograph when the intern emcee introduced me next as a "fat guy on stage for the first time". As if I didn't need a bigger hole to dig myself out of, or it was just my nerves, I had some delusional thought that if I did a dirty set, Dice would fall in love with my act and take me on the road with him. Needless to say, I bombed and died a heroic, horrible death on stage that day. There were two people left in the audience by the time I was through. One was the girl that brought me to this Lion's Den...and she was sound asleep.

I was severely humbled that day. You would think most normal human beings would quit after that experience, but I'm not that normal. It was somewhat fascinating that the stand-up comedy bug would hit me just when I bombed so badly, but during the three hours I was waiting to go on stage, I met a lot of people who were very compelling. It was just not a good time for me professionally or socially but being with these people was sort of escapism. So, even after that experience, I kept going to open mics and soon decided to become a full-fledged stand-up comic.

CHAPTER 2

Al Martin's
Golden Rules of Comedy

started getting obsessed with comedy and decided to immerse myself in the scene because that's how I usually do things. Year later, when I got into Poker I would buy every book and watch every TV show until my head was exploding Poker. I did the exact same thing with Comedy. I started going to open–mics, going to various shows, and watching it on TV obsessively. It was the beginning of the age of the Stand–Up Comedy Specials, and I immersed myself in everything "Comedy".

What else did I have to do? I had no relationship and business was going badly in another line of work that I was in. This brings up one of Al Martin's "Golden Rules of Comedy": He or she, who has the least going on in their life, has the best chance to succeed. During my years in comedy I met lawyers, doctors, surgeons, and judges, who all wanted to become comedians, but it was difficult for them to really succeed since you had to almost live and breathe comedy. People in those professions or 'better' professions tend to have a life and activities outside of comedy; they're used to having a social life and a dating life. They're probably paying off student loans and mortgages, so they can't afford to stop their lives to become performers since being a performer guarantees at least five or six years of poverty, if not a lifetime.

So, having no relationship or anything really going on, it was the perfect time for me to try comedy. I did have one thing going on, however, a beautiful child, who at the time I started in comedy was five years old, so I certainly had to have some concern for things like braces, clothing, and child-support. I did actually have a little bit more to worry about when I was starting, but not quite as much as others who were carrying a lot of baggage like professional careers.

 Living in New York City was very important. I lived in Brooklyn at the time so I was only one subway ride away from being able to do open-mics. I always say the farther out you are in the suburbs, the harder it is to make it as a comedian, because there are less open-mics and fewer opportunities. Add this to my Golden Rules of Comedy: The lighter you travel and the closer you are to a metropolitan area, the better an opportunity you have to make it as a comedian. Those who don't have any great day jobs or any great aspirations or they're living in their parents' basement or anything like that have a much better chance than someone living in the suburbs who has a great day job or who might not yet be ready to commit to a life of poverty.

I started hitting as many open-mics as I could and quickly learned what it means to be an open miker; it means sitting through two hours of other people's terrible acts just so you can do five minutes of your own, but I kept at it. Another tenet of the Al Martin Golden Rules is: Open-mics are not only to be used for working on your set. (I always love these comedians that come over to me and say: "I'm beyond open-mics.") You're never beyond open-mics. I remember doing my Monday open-mic at New York Comedy Club one time and Damon Wayans came in. He had to do Letterman the next night and he was just hungry to run through his set in as many places as he could to get it right. I've had top-flight comedians come into open-mics and run their quick set not only for the Letterman Show, but The Daily Show or whatever they were working on, so I have to chuckle at these two year "veterans" who give me that line, "I'm way beyond open-mics and Bringer shows."

Back to my point, open-mics should not only be used for working on your act, they should also be used for networking and to socialize. This can be rough because most comics are socially inept and socially awkward. They don't know how to talk to people and they don't know how to really open a good line of communication with others.

Why is this important, you ask? It's important because you get to talk to comedians and they will let you know where there might be a good open-mic or there might be an open-mic with an audience. Back in the day when I started, the open-mics in Manhattan were horrific.

There was a place called the Old Triple across from Studio 54. The open mics were on Fridays and Saturdays at midnight, so you can imagine what kind of a rowdy crowd it was! It was a tight space and I remember there were dart games where the darts would go flying past the coach's head. Interestingly, years later I would open Broadway Comedy Club just one block away from the Old Triple.

I've done open-mics in some pretty wacky places and many times it's just an audience of comics staring at you. When you can find an open-mic with an actual audience, it's something very special. It turned out that the best open-mics for that were in the suburbs. I would go to a Wednesday open-mic at Pips Comedy Club in Brooklyn. Sometimes a Tuesday or Wednesday open-mic in Long Island at Chuckles (which was a great club in Mineola) and on Sunday nights a club in Westchester named Shooting Stars. Now mind you, in those days I didn't have a car. I couldn't afford it. I would use mass transit to get to these places and it was quite a trip, but I was committed to comedy. I would take a subway to Grand Central Station and then from Grand Central Station I would grab a train up to Yonkers; then I'd hail a cab, or I'd meet another comedian that had a car. We'd finally get to the venue and then wait hours to eventually do a spot.

You've got to be creative and work outside-of-the-box when you're getting your set stage time. I'd get to Pips at eight to sign up for the open-mic that didn't start till 9:30. What was great about their open-mic is that they mixed it in with a lot of audience members. A couple of pros would always come in and do spots as well. The first few times I got there, I wouldn't get up till 12:30 or 1:00 in the morning.

Of course I had to be ready the next day for work so I made it my strategy to befriend the emcee. One time as I was talking to him he was telling me about some financial issues he had and needed to borrow money. I didn't have a lot of money but I did see this as an opportunity and lent him twenty bucks. That week I got up third instead of thirty-third. Twenty bucks to save three hours of my life seemed like a pretty good deal! A week later I came back to the same open-mic and a lot of people were ahead of me on the line. Another person might have badgered the emcee and asked: "Hey dude, where's my twenty bucks?" Instead when he came over to me, I ask: "Are you okay this week? Do you need another twenty bucks?" and he responds: "I could really use another twenty bucks." So I'd give him another twenty bucks, and again I got up third or fourth that night and I started to realize an important point: sometimes bribery works but we can't call it "bribery". It's called a "loan". This was a lesson that served me in my life – not necessarily the bribery aspect, but thinking outside-of-the-box to get stage time.

Going to open-mics was my catalyst for meeting people. One person I met was a guy by the name of Tim Andre Davis.

Tim was operating a room called the Eagle Tavern and here's another Al Martin rule: If you don't have people to bring to shows and you don't have a way to be contributing audience members to a producer, make yourself useful in another way.

Tim Davis had me do one of his shows and kept telling me what a wonderful comic I was. Of course I was buying those lines of praise at the time because I needed that attention. I soon realized that I wasn't that funny yet, but I did have the ability to come to his shows and help him find people, or help at the box office. Tim would always ask me if I ever ran into any people at other open-mics would I please recommend them for his comedy class. So when I started doing all these helpful things Tim started giving me spots on his shows at The Eagle Tavern and The China Chalet. I eventually started working more and more Tim Davis' shows until he found another room called "Houlihan's". Houlihan's was at 42nd and Lexington in Manhattan and it was where my own comedy career would officially begin.

CHAPTER 3

Huffin' and Puffin' and Going for the Gold

Tim Davis and Ed Stanley ran The Eagle Tavern, China Chalet and Houlihan's. The China Chalet was a one-nighter room and although I was getting most of my stage time at the Eagle Tavern, I was helping Tim run the shows at Houlihan's.

I'd seat people, set up the stage and the microphones, work the box office, do a set, basically a bit of everything. It's where I sort of got my chops working as a comedy show producer. I also helped him get new talent for his shows so they would help bring in audience. This was the beginning of what would later evolve into the "Bringer Show".

As fate would have it, Tim Davis broke his leg and he couldn't continue to show up so I was pretty much running the room alone. After about three months of doing this Tim still was not showing up and I discovered he was running a music night at the Eagle Tavern. I told Tim, "Listen, I don't mind doing this but I'm doing just about everything here and I'd like to be in as a partner even if I have to put up money," (which I didn't have. Why would that stop me?) Tim agreed and I became a partner at the Houlihan's room. I expanded it a bit as well. Each night after the Stand–up Comedy would be over, a DJ would come in and we'd have Singles' Nights. One week they were Christian singles, or Jewish or Latinos. The Comedy Show would morph into one long fun evening. This goes along for a year or so and every week we'd have forty to sixty people showing up. A nice chunk of change for a single Dad.

The day came when Houlihan's told me they're not doing Stand–Up Comedy shows anymore. The manager explained that they had a Reggae Concert the night before and there had been a riot. Management decided they don't want any outside produced shows anymore at the venue. This was three hours before the show and I had sixty people and a dozen comedians on their way with nowhere to put them.

At this point in my life, this was my sole source of income. I sprang into action. I started walking down to 2nd Avenue and 3rd Avenue and walked about ten blocks up, a huffing, puffing, determined Devil, with gunpowder in my soul, and one target only: "A Room". I started working my way down until at 48th Street and 2nd avenue, I found a bar called O'Lunny's. On the first floor was an Irish bar and on the second floor they had a party room that was used at times for overflow for their restaurant. I asked the guy behind the bar (trying not to appear desperate): "Do you have anything up the stairs on the second floor? Would you mind if I brought you sixty people in about two hours?" I thought the guy was gonna come in his pants. He told me he'd love to have sixty fresh customers but he didn't have a waitress.

It turned out by luck one of the comics on the show was not only a New York City school teacher by day, but a waitress part-time at night. So I pitched her. Then I ran straight back to Houlihan's like a breathless fat bat-out-of-hell and I asked her: "Would you like to do a spot tonight but also waitress and make some extra money?" She said yes so I pulled up with my car and my girlfriend at that time helped me load the mics, the speakers and everything we had. We set up shop on 48th and 2nd. I managed to save the show.

Those sixty people packed the place. At the end of the night the bartender, who was also the owner, told me that we were welcome to come back next week and the week after that. We packed the room again and again, week after week, adding a second show on Saturdays; then on Fridays. One of the interns was a young guy named Chris Mazzilli. (Chris eventually went on to open the legendary Gotham Comedy Club.)

Thursday nights became "College Night" and then we added a Wednesday with Jim Mendrinos. (Jim was one of the best comics on the New York circuit and a respected writer who now has his own production company.) He did new material Wednesdays where we brought in comics from all over who would try their material out. On Tuesday nights Steve Aarons developed a show where we served pasta and comedy. On Tuesdays and Mondays the open–mic would start at 5 PM and run until 10 PM. There were probably seventy comics going up through that open–mic. On Sunday nights we developed an Improv Night where we had various Improv Troupes going up.

The Comedy Club had three partners: Tim Davis, Eddie Stanley and me. I would work Sunday through Thursday at the club, handling the phones, bartending, doing whatever I had to do at that time; on Friday and Saturday when I'd be picking up road gigs. Eddie Stanley was running the club and Tim was managing the music world for us. We decided to call it The New York Comedy Club.

We were upstairs at O'Lunny's, yet outside the club was an additional, smaller sign on the awning saying "The New York

Comedy Club". One night I was overcome with the feeling that there were strong vibes in this room, and that I had somehow been summoned. I discovered that in the late 1950s and early 1960s, it was known as the "Living Room" which had a comedy pedigree even back then. It had been a music lounge nightclub and the house band guy was Tony Bevacqua and the house comedian was a guy named Rodney Dangerfield. Together they formed a friendship and eventually opened Dangerfield's on 61st and 2nd in the early 1960s. Dangerfield's was built just like room here –the old New York Comedy Club – with paneling throughout and banquette chairs – a certain late 1950s–60s style. I'll never forget in the last year of The Tonight Show with Johnny Carson when Rodney Dangerfield was one of the guests. He was working out his spots all around town and he did a spot at The New York Comedy Club and when he walked in the door he says: "I recognize this place. I've been here before!" Yup. Twenty years before. This very room had been the old "Living Room" that Cindy Adams had written about.

Even more recently, I didn't realize that there had been an open-mic there, a few weeks prior to the day I took over, and I had arrived late for signup time. No wonder it felt familiar. The guy at the front door was extremely rude to me and said: "What do you think you are? Some kind of prima donna trying to do a spot on an open-mic and showing up late?" I replied that I'm only five minutes late and I'm very sorry of course. (I used the time-worn excuse about the subways being delayed, and thirty years later people still use that excuse with me...not that subways don't get delayed. They do, just not 24 hours a day, 365 days a year!)

And who ran the room back then? Barry Katz, the man who was destined to become the producer of "Last Comic Standing". Barry was one of the most successful men in the business, but not in this room. His attempt to make this room successful failed. This room was mine. Well, not exactly, mine. Not yet.

Barry Katz didn't need this room or the old awning outside with the name "The New York Comedy Club". He owned The

Boston Comedy Club on West 3rd in the village and it became a legendary venue where comics like Dave Chappelle and Sarah Silverman, Marc Maron, Todd Berry, Dave Attelll, Tony Woods and DC Benny learned their craft.

Anyway, The New York Comedy Club was a hit in those early days and we brought in a young guy named Chris Murphy. He was a shift manager over at the legendary Improv Comedy Club. He was working for Silver Friedman and he started telling a lot of the improv acts about this new little club that opened up on 2nd Avenue and he started bringing over a lot of their acts: guys like Marc Cohen and Mike Ivy, Dan Vitale, Dave Attelll, Mike Royce, and a whole bunch of other guys. So we really were the new kid on the block at the time and it was ironic because we opened this club with almost no money and four blocks away from us, some people had spent upwards of $600,000, I heard to open a club called "Rags to Riches" which very quickly went from riches to rags going out of business quite quickly.

It seemed quite perfect except that after a period of time, we were giving Tim his third of the money for the New York Comedy Club, but he was not giving us our two-thirds of the money for the music venue. His debt to us piled up over a period of weeks and finally Tim Davis said: "You guys can keep that dumpy little room on 48th and 2nd. I'll keep the Eagle Tavern for the music show." So in one of the all-time great business moves on my part and maybe one of the worst on Tim's part, we made that deal. Stanley and I became the sole owners of the New York Comedy Club. That would change just a short time later.

CHAPTER 4

Robbery, Regrets and Chris Mazzilli

Our management team was set. I was working Sunday to Thursdays and doing road gigs trying to develop as a comic. Eddie Stanley was handling our weekends. Chris Mazzilli was interning for us and would work, filling shifts, managing and helping out on the weekends. We also added Cheryl Saltzman as a telemarketer to help us procure audience. We were full-time in the comedy business going up against the likes of "Catch a Rising Star" and "The Improv" on the West side.

Chris Murphy, a good friend of mine, would bring acts over from other clubs when he was a part-time manager at The Improv. I said to Chris one day: "Why do all these comics tell me stories about these other club owners but I never hear anybody ever talking about me?" I remember Chris replying: "That's a good thing buddy. You'll stay under the radar." Years later I would appreciate those words when a series of controversies would ultimately surround me.

My social life was non-existent, but I really enjoyed this extremely busy period in my life. I was focused and constantly trying to improve as a comedian, hence another Al Martin Rule of Comedy: Find a Headliner who needs a ride somewhere. There's an anecdote about a comic who wanted to be booked. He would ask the booker: "Do you need a headshot?" And the Booker would reply: "No! Just send me a picture of your car."

One night Bob Golub struts into the club real cocky (with a long-haired Rich Vos). Bob was right out of Central Casting for the role of some purple head from the steel mills of

Pennsylvania – a tough He–Man type, and we were about as different as two people could be. Bob was a real Redneck, an "in–shape" guy who had a brief career as a boxer and spent time in prison; I was a fat kid from Brooklyn. Bob asked me if I would work with him on the road. "I need an opener this weekend in Washington DC." He was playing a Comedy Club Chain called "Garvin's" which back then was a well known comedy club chain in the mid–Atlantic area of the country with twelve locations. It would pay $200 for the weekend. I was glad to get the experience. It was my first decent paying gig, even though it's really just $50 a show. Today, a lot of comedians would tell you to go to hell if you asked them to drive you to Washington DC for $50.00 per show. I had never been to DC and it was a chance for a whole new experience in my fledgling comedy career.

I drove Bob to DC, and we had four wacky shows. The Emcee, Patton Oswalt, was at the time just a local act but was destined for stardom, earning such roles as Spencer Olchin in "The King of Queens" and the narrator in "The

Goldbergs". Bob and I developed a friendship which still exists today. The owner of the club, Don Siegel, was a character in his own way. He befriended me because he was another Jewish kid from Long Island. We got to talking and he said: You did a very good job. I'd like to bring you back to work one of my other rooms." He said he'd pay me the same salary I was getting this weekend...$500!

There I was, thinking how fortunate I was to find a comedian who worked on the road and would help me get into other rooms, but Bobby was playing his own game with me, although he denies it to this day. But consider this: I never really minded because that was the deal I made with him. I was happy with the $200. Of course I was a lot happier with $500, but I was just fine that weekend with the $200. It got me exactly what I wanted, an "entranceway" where the owner saw that I was capable of doing the job. I wound up getting a lot of work. Garvin's was a very big deal at the time. I got to meet some other comics like Sam Greenfield. Even though I initially took a beating from the pay, the experience became a cornucopia of good luck. Don Siegel introduced me to Anne Kiel from Florida who booked me in a room called the Hollywood Comedy Club in Hollywood Beach, Florida. My father, who had no real money, would bring the family down in the summers when it was hot as hell and cheap, but this was my first time to Florida as a sane adult.

Anne Kiel liked the job I did in Florida at Uncle Funny's and The Hollywood Beach Comedy Club so she booked me at Jesters in Trump Castle, Atlantic City (now the Golden Nugget). Like every other ego–maniac, I was thrilled to see my name on a marquee and all over the lobby in Atlantic City. It was a dream come–true.

One day I was in the steam room at The Trump Marina Casino, and in walks Al Martino, the singer from The Godfather movie (the character who's rival woke up next to a horse's severed head). I said: "You're Al Martino?" He nods. "My name is Al Martin. I've been performing in the comedy club all week and I've been getting a lot of your calls."

"What do you mean?" he asked

"Well," I reply, "I'm getting calls from Sally from Brooklyn, and Angie from Bay Ridge, and Vic from Bensonhurst. They're all calling me up at all hours of the day and night saying: Allie boy, how are you?"

And he goes: "Well better you than me pal! I don't know any of these people and I'm glad you're getting my calls! Welcome to showbiz!"

Bob Golub decided to head out to Los Angeles to seek fame and fortune as many comics do. He was hoping to get a sitcom and he was an incredible comedian worthy of great success. A guy named Ross Mark befriended Bob in Los Angeles. Bob told him about the Toupee I wore which Bob hated. When we'd travel on the road, Bob would do all sorts of silly things like hide the toupee five minutes before I had to go onstage. That toupee was like a security blanket to me. Bob hated it. One day he deliberately ejaculated into the toupee rendering it a mess and permanently useless. Into the garbage it went. Ross Mark was revolted, yet intrigued. The toupee story got him. He just happened to be the Producer of "Evening at The Improv".

I also got a week out in Vegas to perform and again saw my name up in lights – in Vegas! Within two years or so of driving a Headliner 300 miles for a measly $50 per night gig, (which many other comics scoffed at), I was playing in Atlantic City, Vegas, and the legendary Improv stage in LA . Not to mention that I met Budd Friedman!

It was really a whirlwind couple of years...a great memory... except for one major regret which haunts me to this day and involves Chris Mazzilli.

Ross Mark asked me to refer some comics from the East coast for what would turn out (unbeknownst to me) to be the final "Evening of the Improv" show. I recommended three comics: Mike King, Gary Greenberg, a very talented and brilliant performer who went on to become head writer on the Jimmy Kimmel show (who had interned at The New York

Comedy Club) and Chris Mazzilli, who not only did a superior job of managing The New York Comedy Club, but was a pretty good comedian. They were thrilled. The show was canceled, however, just at that point, and they only had spots for two comics for the final show – not four. They chose Mike King and told me it was my choice who the second comic would be. I selfishly chose to do that spot myself...and in so doing, I disappointed and pissed off two great guys. But that's not all. I managed to infuriate Chris Mazzilli even more.

Back at the New York Comedy Club, I was starting to get suspicious tallies from my partner Eddy. The figures for the nights he was working always seemed to be off. It just wasn't sitting right with me based on how large the audiences were and what other comics were telling me. I had a meeting with Eddy and decided that we probably needed to lay off either Cheryl or Chris because based on his reported figures we just couldn't afford it. Chris and Cheryl were concerned about their jobs and showed me the figures they had written down which were far different than Eddy's ....

I had another meeting with Eddy and when we were done he stepped down and I took over full control of The New York Comedy Club. My partner had not been totally forthcoming with me. If it weren't for Chris, I may not have known this. I was extremely grateful to Chris for his diligence in letting me know the actual numbers and I substantially increased his salary, but Chris wanted more. I think he wanted to be my new partner.

Instead Chris Mazzilli went on to open The Gotham Comedy Club, a beautiful, highly–regarded venue! However, it took years for the rift to be healed.

CHAPTER 5

Steak, Suspicions, and Success

Imagine if you will an Argentinian steakhouse by day and an after-hours social club by night. A basement replete with broken slot machines, used condoms, and a Danny DeVito clone for a landlord. The happy still-lingering stench of illicit activity by famous athletes and hockey players who used the basement as an after-hours playground. What better place to relocate The New York Comedy Club than this 125 year-old tenement style building on a quiet, dark side-street on 24th and 2nd? What better spot to welcome celebrities who had frequented the place in its former incarnation? They would look around, wide-eyed and ask: "Didn't I eat steak here?" It seemed like paradise ...at first.

One afternoon these two young dreamers, Mark Wingington and Emerson Macoute, approached me to hire them. In those days, tickets were sold over the phone, advertised in the newspaper, or through repeat customers. They had the outrageously silly idea to carry a poster in Times Square and sell comedy tickets. They were willing to work on commission. I thought to myself that these guys are talking out of their ass. They must be borderline crazy. They had pitched this idea to a few different clubs and were rejected by all of them. That did it for me. Give me an "underdog" anytime. I'll give him a chance especially when I have nothing to lose.

Those two guys revolutionized how people would buy comedy tickets. They had an almost cult–like crew of sales people that would get to the club at around 10 AM to pick up tickets, yell and scream rally songs to get psyched, go out to Times Square for hours, sell a shitload of tickets and then, after a long day, head to the arcade to play games. A new breed of salesman had entered the scene. Before them we were lucky to get twenty phone calls per day. Suddenly the phone rang nonstop. This also attracted great comedians because New York Comedy Club was getting a reputation as a room that always had a packed house.

The neighbors fiercely hated the club. You would think that we would be a good presence on a dark, silent street. A lit-up business, a few chatting comedians, some late night audience members, all serve to make people feel more secure, right? Around that time, New York City implemented a 311 policy where people can call 311 and make various complaints. I think they waited for my club to open. They were flooded with complaints immediately and one complainer was relentless.

I tried everything from inviting them to comedy shows or hosting block parties and always speaking to them with reverential respectful tones. But, for the entire twenty years we were there, the neighbors just wanted us out.

One Saturday evening at around 6 PM (a relatively slow time for comedy clubs) an entire Swat Team arrived and came flying out of an armored truck. They swarmed the club. My daughter Melinda (who's all of 4 foot 11) was managing. They pushed her aside (albeit gently) and said they were here to investigate numerous complaints, and stormed into the showroom. There was an Improv Comedy Show and just six audience members, who were, needless to say a bit startled. "I know we suck," said one of the comics, "but I didn't know we were that bad." Disappointed and dejected the Swat Team walked out leaving a few low level unsubstantial fines. But Ms. Relentless continued to complain.

The landlord seemed like a decent guy. The man he purchased the building from, on the other hand, was steeped in mystery. We called him the Godfather.

He had a special deal with my landlord to keep a "Social Club" next door to the venue. His associates would park their limousines, come up and kiss his hand. Sometimes it would be a day–long procession. At the end of the day they. would lock up his club and his caretaker would wheel him down the block to a luxury apartment building. He was always nice to me and it seemed innocent enough. Ms.Relentless didn't agree. She demanded a full investigation from the city.

This guy had to be someone. I didn't know who and I didn't want to delve too deeply into his suspicious life–style.

The city building inspector arrives and, as it turns out, back when The Godfather owned the building, he cemented the floor of the entire backyard. He built an illegal room on the cement connecting it to the front area of the place, obviously. without obtaining any necessary permits from the city. This illegal structure on the. strange cement floor became part of the Argentinian Steakhouse. And for years nobody seemed to care a lick about it until a year after it became The New York Comedy Club.

We were ordered by the city to take down the original structure and build a new one in its place. This had to be done in record time to satisfy the city's building requirements. It was not required that the cement floor be dug up, and to this day no one knows for sure what might lie beneath.

Knowing none of this at the time, I had been thrilled to sign the lease. Normally when a person leases a space and the landlord takes your security deposit, you assume that the place is legal with all its necessary permits. In fact, it is the landlord's responsibility to ensure that. When a problem arises, one assumes the landlord will pick up the entire cost of putting up the new building, since it is his building. Not so with my landlord. I was presented with a bill for $14,000, one half of the estimated cost to build the new structure. But just to be fair, he'd allow me to pay it off in installments over two years by adding it to my rent. What a guy.

Even though I would find out several years later that the ENTIRE cost of putting up the structure was only $14,000, I reluctantly agreed. The New York real estate market at the time was hot and I didn't want to start the search for a new place. The rent was actually cheap and business was good. If my middle name wasn't Santa Claus, it was Shmuck.

It was at this time that my manager Chris Mazziili asked to privately meet with me and his investment banker friend named Mike Reisman, who was into producing comedy shows. Chris asked me if I would be willing to sell the New York comedy club to Mike and him. I was finally making a living at the comedy club and enjoying it. I politely declined.

A few days later I came to the club and noticed that my desk was broken in half on the floor. I found my bus boy Mike Bocchetti (Mike went on to co-host the Artie Lange radio show and to be a finalist on NBC 's last Comic Standing). I asked Mike what happened to my desk? Mike is well-known to stutter and stammer when he's nervous. He withstood my grilling for all of one minute, when he reluctantly confessed that Chris Mazzilli broke the desk while he was banging a chick in my office. This was alarming because this was a puzzling departure from his natural self. Chris was always a straight-laced, serious guy. He would never indulge in banging someone on a desk and leaving it broken. Two weeks later Chris gave me his notice of resignation. He and the same Mike Reisman partnered together to open what would become The Gotham Comedy Club.

The glory years at The New York Comedy Club cascaded in. All sorts of celebrities loved to stop in and watch the shows: Tennis great Andre Agassi, James Farentino, Louise Lasser. Michael Douglas would bring his father Kirk to watch his brother Eric do standup.

Then there were the celebs who wanted to pursue a stand-up comedy career... Elizabeth Ray (known in the late 70s as the secretary who couldn't type) was involved in the first major sex scandal where Congressman Wayne Hays was booted from Congress; Wrestler Johnny Valiant, who also became an tag team champion and a famous announcer/manager in wrestling; and real estate developer and perennial mayoral candidate Abe Hirschfeld, all stood onstage at The New York Comedy Club to hone their stand-up skills. Every one of them quit. The work, the dedication, the struggle it takes to make it, baffled them. Comedy can be very humbling no matter how much money you have to throw at it. It is probably the toughest job in entertainment. But for those who were determined, The New York Comedy Club was there.

CHAPTER 6

The Comedy World Stole All My Ideas

Call me low-brow. Call me classless. Call me whatever the fuck you want to call me, but my original ideas are now part of every comedy club in Manhattan and many throughout the country. I thought of them first. These ideas are mine and I hereby lay claim to them. Here's the first:

The Bringer Show: One night a couple of comics were hanging at the bar during an open-mic and they asked me if they could work our regular house show for the evening. I politely said they'd have to outshine the comics that I was already putting up. Maybe one day they would achieve that status, but at that point each of them needed a lot more experience and stage time. Five minutes at open–mics performing for other comics, or waiting for hours to get on after regular shows for a short time, wasn't cutting it for them. You might recognize this scrappy group of open mikers today as Bill Hicks, Todd Barry, Dave Attell, Louis CK, and Brett Butler. Then they asked me:

"If we can put together a show and bring our own audience, would you be open to letting us do a show at an off–hour?"

I thought about it and I said:"Why not?" A few days later, on a weekday night, the room had fifty customers. The bell in my head started ringing. Why not do this regularly? Why not do this twice a night, several times a week? Why not enable new comics to get up there and learn their craft? Of course when the glittering glistening clubs discovered I was doing this, they scoffed at me. I was told that the Bringers show is exploitive. I, however, was delighted to be considered comedy club scum. Their arrogance and blind–sightedness fueled my sense of competition and on certain days when their clubs were dark, mine was packed. Eventually they stole my idea and made the concept mainstream. All the clubs in Manhattan that didn't follow suit eventually folded.

Performing a lot is the only way a comic improves. I couldn't expose them to a Saturday night audience yet. Rather than standing on stage in front of just a few people at 2AM, the bringers loved performing to a packed house and a real audience. I was giving them a platform to perform and I'm the one who pays rent to a Landlord for their opportunity. How is that exploitive?

Comics would ask what happens when they run out of friends? First, read this book and follow the Al Martin Golden Rules of Comedy. Secondly, read it again. Befriend a comedy show producer. Help out. Check people in at the door. Clean the tables. Sweep. Produce your own show and swap spots. Substitute for others sometimes when asked. In any other business, opportunity presents itself when you really want to achieve something. Comedy is no different. Many of our Bringers went on to big success: Jocelyn Chia,

Leigh Ann Lord, John Fugelsang and Fox News morning host Brian Kilmeade. The list goes on and on.

But there's always the new comic who haughtily states with 'their nose way up in the air' that he or she would never do a Bringer show. The comic will insist he or she "is better than that." They look down on the comics doing Bringer shows. Really? My patent response is: "With very little experience, do you think you would be ready to make a 9PM lineup at a show in Manhattan without crumbling on the stage or without wearing a raincoat for the metaphoric tomatoes thrown at your face? Just ask Joan Rivers." I'm not referring to a bar show which is basically a circle jerk in front of the same fifteen comics every week. I'm referring to a real life club with 200 people from various places in the country sitting in a room, with varied dialects and levels of understanding. Do your jokes fall flat with some people? Do you know how to call up another one quickly? If you can't do that, if you can't make people laugh consistently and loudly, if the answer is "no" then you're not ready to comment about people who do Bringer shows.

A dirty little secret that should be committed to memory by all aspiring comics: If all Bringer shows were eliminated tomorrow, half the comedy clubs in Manhattan would be out of business!

So....if you can't bring yourself to be a 'Bringer' then thank the muses of comedy that there are others who will!" Most, if not 'all' Comedy Clubs are open and doing business because there are new comics who initially participate in Bringer shows. Some may be hobbyists, people who do comedy as a lark and have real jobs during the day. They want to get their five minutes on stage and they can't sit in some bar for hours until they get on stage in front of twelve people. They may even be a Dentist who will pull your tooth one day, or a Lawyer who will get you out of your DUI. Business is a cycle and we all help each other out. In other words, shut your fucking mouth about Bringers. They are an absolute necessity. Theses shows are sometimes called New

Talent, or Emerging Artists, or whatever, but they are a fundamental Building block and often help keep the clubs open for the big nights.

Industry Shows – My Original Invention: Beyond the Tonight Show bookers, beyond the Stephen Colbert or Conan O'Brien Show bookers, lie the On–The–Road bookers, The Out–of–Town nightclub bookers, the Corporate Gigs, and the High–end–party bookers, and for this target group I created the "Industry Show". This subset of bookers are brought to our club, and they are able to find exactly which comics they want for their event.

Why Stop at Comedy Shows? There was only one type of comedy club show when I first came on the scene in Manhattan – a 9:00 PM show and perhaps a late show on the weekends. I was the only comedy club owner to open up my stages to Improve shows, Cabaret shows and full–blown plays and musicals. There were all kinds of performers who wanted an audience. Entrepreneurs abounded. My interest in marketing strategies kept prodding me on to more.

Theme Shows: In the mid 1990s I approached comedian Seymour Swan, and together we started New York's top African-American comedy show. This ran weekly and was the longest running shows of its kind. How could we miss with the likes of Wanda Sykes, Damon Wayans, Kevin Hart, and Tracy Morgan? In 1996 I started Latino Laughter with Ozzie Baez, which included Angel Salazar and Andrew Kennedy. The New York Comedy Club also hosted New York's funniest Gay and Lesbian comedians way before anybody else did.

Two Rooms: The New York Comedy Club became the first room in the history of New York City to have two show rooms. I used to like to call the second room the "bowling alley" because it was a very long narrow room. Comics would go from room to room to do a set. It was heaven with liquor. Today, many comedy clubs are copying what I pretty much invented twenty years ago.

Things were going so well that Don Siegel invited me to partner with him at the Boconuts Comedy Club in Boca

Raton, Florida. I welcomed the opportunity. The name, of course, would be changed to "The New York Comedy Club" but this time there was no Chris Mazzilli to be my manager. We were in for a ride.

CHAPTER 7

Just Like Steinbrenner

There was a glorious time in Manhattan in the late 1960s and the early 1970s for comedy clubs like "Catch a Rising Star"; "Dangerfields"; "The Comic Strip"; and "The Improv" when the manager would unlock the door and eager audiences would rush in. Two million potential customers with just four comedy clubs meant large audiences waiting outside and joyously filling up every seat at every table, drinks in their hands and smiles on their dollar–sign faces. It was a splendid chunk of time for comedy club owners – an era that would abruptly end. In 1994, Catch a Rising Star filed for bankruptcy and went out of business, The Improv Comedy Club collapsed soon after. In a growing city like Manhattan their business tactics were archaic. They couldn't survive.

In the early 90's there was an ensuing ground war in the comedy club scene but there was nothing really funny about it. The Comedy Cellar and The Boston Comedy Club opened in The Village; Stand–Up New York opened on the upper Westside, Carolines moved to the South Seaport from Chelsea, and of course, my little New York Comedy Club on 24th Street had its own niche. Within a few years the number of comedy clubs had doubled in New York. It took, however, more than just a " room with fake brick walls" to survive. The comedy climate dramatically changed. A multitude of new comics of all ages wanted stage–time. Some were destined to make it big, and only those clubs who would work in tandem with that vital energy force would survive.

Catch a Rising Star and The Improv never wanted to be involved in the new talent business. When Catch a Rising Star reinvented itself in 1996, with the label: "An Art and Entertainment Center" (in direct competition with Chris

Mazzilli's: "The Gotham Comedy Club") everyone bet on their success except me. I knew that enigmatic label would doom the club. It had no focus or identity. How would anyone know that it was a comedy club? Gotham Comedy Club sky-rocketed to success while "Catch" crashed and burned. "Catch" however, bequeathed me an invaluable guy – Rich Brooks – who came along just when I needed him. He would prove to be invaluable as a friend and producer for years to come.

I answered the phone one day in 2001, and lo and behold it was Barry Katz (The creator of 'Last Comic Standing'). He was a busy guy who managed Dave Chapelle and Jay Mohr at the same time he was operating "The Boston Comedy Club" in Greenwich Village. When his managing surrogates moved to Los Angeles, a management team was needed immediately at The Boston Comedy Club. They reached out to me. I became the first person in New York history to operate two comedy clubs simultaneously.

Ego is a constant companion of comedians and club owners alike. It follows them wherever they go and spurs them as often to exceptional heights as it incites them to ridiculous over-reaction. Such was the case with Dustin Chafin. Dustin had once been my shift manager at The New York Comedy Club on 24th Street. We had a vicious, spitfire, terrible falling-out and he walked out. I can't remember a single detail of the argument. Not one. I don't know if I was wrong or if he was wrong. But I knew I liked him and he did the job well. I asked him to be the Comedy Club booker at The Boston Comedy Club. Fortunately he accepted.

It's okay to have a difference of opinions. It's okay to argue. It's okay for me to fire a server who gives away free drinks to her friends. Employees are human and they sometimes do the wrong thing. But often they change. They grow. I would fight with a lot people through the years and have a falling out. Somehow, after weeks or months or years, I would welcome them back into the Al Martin sphere. Without words really, all would be forgiven in what would become a recurring theme in this business. Chris Murphy was prompted to call me the "George Steinbrenner of Comedy". In that spirit, I was delighted to bring Dustin Chafin back.

Business at The Boston Comedy Club was humming along. Rich Brooks was handling the New Talent shows, Dustin Chafin was booking the comics, and I was handling the marketing. All was good for about a year and a half until New York property skyrocketed in value. The property was sold to NYU for additional dorm space. The Boston Comedy Club was demolished. Along with the disappearance of The Improv and Catch a Rising a Star, New York was losing a great part of its comedy identity.

But that would not last for long.

CHAPTER 8

Artie Lange A Big Boca Hero

To a lot of people Artie Lange is a funny comedian with an inextricable drug problem that has disfigured his face. But to me, Artie Lange is a hero. I first met Artie in 1992. He was a member of Improv Troupe The Improbables. This was years before his career surged, years before Mad TV and years before he became Howard Stern's sidekick. He came into my lobby that first night, nudged my arm in his uniquely friendly, albeit gruff way, and introduced himself. How could I know, that a decade later, Artie Lange would save my ass?

Artie would appear with Bob Levy at various comedy clubs. Bob Levy, known as "Reverend Bob" was doing standup on the Howard Stern Show. He was hosted by the show's writer, Jackie Martling. Martling gave Levy the nickname "The

Reverend" as Levy says, "because I was a filthy fuckin' pig, and he wanted to call me the opposite of what I was doing onstage". When I first started out in comedy, I was not known by anybody. I was not even particularly funny, as happens with all of us comics; it is a learning process like all things. Bob Levy, however, gave me more spots than anyone else. He would book me on tours and great one–nighters.

In the late 1990s I had taken up Don Siegel's offer to partner with him at another New York Comedy Club in Boca Raton, Florida. We took over a venue called Bocanuts and today it's The Boca Black Box. At that time it was a 350 seat room and I initially had a problem filling it because the kind of acts that would fill 350 seats room just weren't available to me and not because I wasn't willing to spend big money. I literally had a "chain" choking my ability to hire big acts: it was called "The Improv".

"The Improv" in Fort Lauderdale made it clear, according to many comedians that that if they worked my venue, or any other venue, they'd be blacklisted from Improvs across the country. They chose not to work for me and I couldn't blame them. But Artie did choose to work at my venue and he was the one that really put that club on the map. If Artie wasn't the kind of performer who had a huge following and inspired other comics to work for me, we may never have survived. Once he worked the New York Comedy Club in Florida, a whole slew of comedians came down: Brett Butler, (from the hit sitcom "Grace Under Fire"), Gilbert Gottfried, Shawn Wayans, and the list went on and on. But Artie was the one that broke open the doors. I'll tell you another thing about Artie Lange. There's never been a charity that needed help that Artie has not put himself out there for. When he was down with his problems, and I would see people make fun of him, it really pissed me off.

One night Artie Lange brought Reverend Bob and another comic, Beetlejuice, to close his show at The New York Comedy Club in Boca. Beetlejuice was an actor and comedian with microcephaly and dwarfism, who was a frequent guest on The Howard Stern Show. As a member of

Stern's Wack Pack, he was named the greatest Wack Packer of all time.

Reverend Bob and Beeetlejuice had a well-loved bit. They would pick a female audience member to stand on stage while Bob Levy applied whip cream to the woman's rump and Beetlejuice would then lick it off. The audience would roar with laughter. One night a girl came in with a date who had gone to the bathroom when she volunteered for this outrageous stunt. When her boyfriend returned he found his date bent over on stage with a little person face first in her ass full of whipped cream. The audience was in stitches. This was the closing bit and the comedians exited backstage to uproarious applause. The boyfriend, enraged, made a beeline towards the dressing room. When I noticed, I rushed toward the back. It was a fucking free-for-all! Fists flying! Passions raging in the middle of a dwarf and Reverend knuckle sandwich!

My partner at the time was Don Siegel. Don happened to be a very principled, down-to-the-penny accurate, accountant.

Don also owned a hair replacement center. Don wore a toupee. Probably the worst toupee in history. You'd look at his toupee and want to feed it.

Don and I finally broke up the fight. The guy left in a huff and my partner noticed that he hadn't paid his tab. He went running into the parking lot and caught up to him, but the guy was in his car with the doors locked ready to flee. Don jumps on the hood and would not let go. The car was revving and bucking – doing doughnuts in the parking lot trying to shake him off!

Don's toupee was flapping in the melee and flew ten feet off his head before eventually getting run over by the car. Don rolled off the hood and the couple sped away. I picked up the toupee and handed it to Siegel. He slapped it back on his head saying: "I guess the secret's out." Sure, Don. It was never a secret. He was wearing the worst toupee in history.

The following Monday Artie Lange told the story on the Stern Show and The New York Comedy Club in Boca Raton began doing business like never before. Artie literally put us on the map.

Needless to say, the furious boyfriend took off and never paid, but the following Monday Artie Lange spoke about this incident on the Howard Stern Show and The New York Comedy Club in Boca Raton began doing business like never before. Artie literally put it on the map. Maybe that girl had whipped cream unexpectedly smeared on her ass by the very strange but endearing Beetlejuice, but, just as unexpectedly, Artie Lange saved mine.

Then they came – all the big names – including Gilbert Gottfried. My wife, Carolyn, and I went to the Fort Lauderdale Airport to pick him up. She was driving. Gilbert and I were standing behind the car to put his luggage in the trunk. My wife was so excited to see Gilbert that she started to get out of the car not realizing it was in "Reverse". Within an inch of running both Gilbert and me over, I yelled to her. She got back in and threw the car into "Park". When his weekend gig was over, I offered him a ride to the airport. "Not if your wife is driving," he retorted.

One Saturday night we couldn't find Pauly Shore for the second show! His first show was a big hit, but no one had a clue where he was. The clock was ticking and no Pauly Shore. It was one minute to show–time. My heart was pounding. I didn't know if he was pissed, lost, drunk, or dead. We stood in the parking light with dread in our hearts not knowing what to do. Suddenly Pauly comes stumbling out of the Asian Massage Parlor two doors down…

Ultimately it was tough for me to run a club in two different states. I didn't like the idea of having a partner and after a few years I sold my interest in the club to Don Siegel. My landlord at The New York Comedy Club had purchased another building near Times Square, and wanted to know if I'd be interested in opening a comedy club there. I honestly couldn't think of anything else I'd rather do.

"Times Square" here comes Al Martin.

CHAPTER 9

Love, Laughs, and Limits

I was that high school kid in the mid 70's who rebelled against typing class. I'd ask "Why do I need to spend hours learning this crap?" Who could foresee that twenty years later the ability to type would bring a wonderful Red-headed girl named Carolyn into my life to share my dreams and my bed?

One night I came home at 2:30 AM, checked on my son David (asleep in his room), settled down in front of my computer, and discovered "Love @AOL", an online dating service. I was attracted to one girl from Rockaway Beach, Queens – we began sending instant messages to each other. The problem is she'd type ten times faster than me.

My work day was atypical and my hours were late. Both Comedy Clubs were in full swing: Florida, and Manhattan. I hired a replacement for Chris Mazzilli – Linda Corke. Linda was tough and experienced. She owned Jimmy's Comedy Alley in Bayside, Queens which had been successful, but ran its course. Linda's expertise was needed. She knew how to structure offers and had lots of connections. She dealt with agents and managers of bigger acts. Even with her help, I needed to be at the club often and stay late.

Frustrated by how slowly I was responding, Carolyn and I decided to speak on the phone. I've always believed there are three factors needed for a relationship to succeed; most people are only aware of the big two – a physical attraction and an emotional connection, but the third which is equally as important is "timing". Between the time I divorced my child's mother and the year 2000, I met a lot of women who could fulfill me physically and emotionally, but the timing was just not right. A few women were ready to take the relationship to the next step, but I was not there yet.

In the 1990s my ex–wife informed me that she was getting divorced from her second husband and since she could not afford a two bedroom apartment, David had to live with me; I would need to take care of him full–time. I was determined to first create a good foundation in my life, and after making some mistakes early on, or being a victim of some bad luck, I had to really create a future for my child and myself.

Relationships, as wonderful as they are, can sometimes hinder you like an albatross around your neck, since it is much easier to make a decision for yourself, go where you want to go, and do what must be done, without having a mate to consult or be concerned with. Another Golden Rule in making it as a comic: "Travel light."

When I decided to dial Carolyn's number that first night, it had been almost fifteen years since I had been married, and at this point the journey had come full circle. I was looking for a person to share my life with. So, when I looked in on my son that night at 2:30 in the morning, I had no idea that he was about to inherit two sisters.

The night I picked her up for our first date, I noticed in my rearview mirror that her oldest daughter Samantha was copying down my license plate number. I started wondering what the hell I was getting into dating a woman with kids. I couldn't know yet the myriad of problems that would ultimately enhance my life and open my eyes to warmth, security and love.

Our first date was in a restaurant in Freeport, Long Island; the food was noticeably bad, but the conversation and connection were great. We were like two dried up sponges, hungry for each other. Needless to say she was late for her teaching job the next morning. After a whirlwind courtship we got married less than a year later. We first had a Civil Service in Las Vegas with Elvis performing wedding songs and drove on the Vegas strip in a pink Cadillac. Then we had a religious ceremony for family in Florida. We were united in the eyes of God.

So, we settled into our own little Brady Bunch world: two daughters named Samantha and Melinda from her previous marriage and my son David. Carolyn's job was in Canarsie, Brooklyn, and I needed access to Manhattan. We set up home in Staten Island. Very cozy. Right? I never thought we would survive the first year of marriage! It was one fight after another. Not only did two independent adults have to learn how to live with each other, not only did both of them have baggage from previous marriages, but we had brought in three adolescent kids to live together under one roof.

The first year was Hell on Earth.

What got us through it? Therapy, therapy, therapy and after all of that, more therapy! I was going to Family Therapy once a week with the whole family. Then I was going to Marriage Counseling with Carolyn once a week, and then I was going to One–on–One counseling to figure out how stupid I was to get myself in this predicament.... I had a nice easy life, a beautiful place to live, a beautiful car, and then I brought this fractured madness onto myself. Just how stupid could I have been?

Something clicked in year two. The family started coming together as a unit, and we all learned a few things: "COMPROMISE"; learning to let go of certain things. For example, in the beginning of the marriage, it drove me nuts to see the kids' bedrooms a mess. I figured out a really sophisticated, complicated technique to deal with this: I made them shut the fucking door. If the door is closed I don't see the mess. It had been a struggle, but we were making it as a family unit.

Then it hit me: with three more mouths to feed I did need to figure out a way to make more money.

CHAPTER 10

The ~~Jackie Mason~~ Improv Comedy Club

Around the time The Boston Comedy Club was closing, my landlord over at The New York Comedy Club (the Danny DeVito clone) approached me about opening a club in Times Square. He purchased a building on 53rd at Eighth Avenue. He had a first floor space that he wanted me to look at. When I got to the space I ascertained that at the rent he wanted, it would be hard to justify a mere seventy-five seat club. As I was walking around the building I noticed a basement. "What are you going to do with the basement?" He said it would probably become a storage area and was dead space. It was three times the size of the upstairs space.

I cut a deal with him to rent three times the space for half the money. This became the mantra for Al Martin math: "Try to get as much space for as little money as possible". Find a space that nobody else would want. And fill the place with laughter.

I consulted Mark Wiggington and Emerson Moncure (who were heading my Street Team) and asked them if they thought they could market both the New York Comedy Club on the East side and this new club. They assured me they could. I rented the space and began what I thought would be an easy venture. It wasn't.

Shortly after signing the lease, I was informed that the school a few doors away was objecting to me getting a Liquor license. They said I was too close to the entrance of their school. I checked New York City maps and found the entrance to the school was actually on 52nd St. and not on my block: 53rd Street. The school claimed, however, that the back exit which was an Emergency Exit, was now going to become an entrance for handicapped students. Their basis for denying me a full Liquor License was that six handicapped children coming in six hours before I open to the public, would somehow be endangered by my serving liquor. They persevered and won. I was forced to open with a Beer and Wine License only. Naysayers shouted that I was doomed to fail. Failure wasn't an option for me, not with a wife and three kids, who were now my responsibility. I had to figure out a way to succeed. I built out this club using every last dime I had.

Every story, every project, every business, needs a good name. A good name helps you to forge forward and overcome obstacles. You see it in yours mind's eye. It beckons you. The problem is I didn't have a name yet.

I was thinking that I could use some star power in the name to be competitive. Jackie Mason is one of my favorite comedians on stage. You have to admire a person who had seven One–Man Broadway shows, who incites a continual flow of belly laughs, and who is legendary. I'm a person who takes food seriously. In my earlier years of comedy, after a long night, I would be at any one of New York's great delis—The Carnegie, the Stage, or Sarges. Jackie was a friendly guy who frequented the same delis as I did late at night, and would come over to the table, and even though he didn't know me, would stick his fork right in my Cole slaw, grab a pickle from my plate, or snatch a slice of pastrami from my sandwich. With his mouth full, he would ask me "Are you Jewish?" This happened maybe ten times throughout the years.

A friend of mine named Marty Fisher suggested I use the name: "The Jackie Mason Comedy Club". He certainly had name recognition. Jackie lived nearby and would undoubtedly be willing to show up occasionally at the club. So I set up a meeting with Jackie Mason and his manager, Jyll Rosenfeld, to discuss licensing his name. It was an amicable meeting. They laid out their terms and I was serious about pulling this deal off.

Just before the deal was finalized, about two weeks later, I was on vacation in Las Vegas with my wife and we decided at the behest of Jackie Mason to see his show at the MGM Casino. In an arena that seats five thousand, there were 300 people in the audience Jackie's management had gotten us great seats all the way up front which afforded us a great view of the people coming into the arena for the show. Maybe seventy percent of them were coming in with walkers, canes, or wheelchairs! This was 2003. I looked at my wife, and said, "In ten years, we're still going to be paying Jackie Mason for his name and chances are none of these people will be attending." It was a bit of a deal breaker. I changed my mind. Of course this did not sit well with Jackie Mason or Jyll Rosenfeld. His next two one–man shows transitioned from Broadway to OffBroadway, but he kept writing, and his audiences kept laughing, even though they were aging.

About a year later, a nineteen–year–old girl asked to work at The New York Comedy Club. I gave her a shot as a server. I then received a phone call from Jackie Mason's attorney asking me, as a personal favor to Jackie, not to employ this young girl because she was falsely claiming that she was

Jackie Mason's daughter and he resented it. I researched the situation and learned that a woman named Ginger Reiter successfully prevailed in a Paternity Suit in Dade County Court in Miami, Florida, in 1988, against Jackie Mason claiming that Jackie had fathered a child. The blood test proved it beyond doubt. He was court-ordered to pay child support. That child was Sheba Mason.

Now even though Jackie and his people denied that he was the father of this child, I closely examined the dated photographs in the papers. Jackie Mason's face was on a child's body. She was the spitting image of her father. The courts called it a "striking resemblance". So when Jackie's attorney muscled me to fire this girl Sheba, I asked, "On what grounds?" The answer was again, "As a personal favor to Jackie." The smoke coming from my ears may have been visible. I'm a pretty hard-headed person from Brooklyn who really didn't decide to get into business thirty years ago to have someone tell me how to operate my business. I wondered what puny spiritual fibers these people must have been made of to ask such a question. A brilliant comedian who not only denies his own child, but didn't want her to work where she pleased? They had the wrong guy. Besides, I'm the world's greatest fan of the "Underdog". I respectfully declined their request.

Buddy Flip, a comedy teacher at The New York Comedy Club, snatched Sheba right up. There was no way in hell she wouldn't become a great comedian. To this day I continue to employ Sheba who became a good friend. Her mother, Ginger Reiter, is a playwright, and as of late, my wife and I perform in Ginger's musicals, including the successful and acclaimed: "The Jackie Mason Musical". It stars Sheba as her own mother, in love with her own father, and pregnant with herself. If baffles even the most astute psychiatrists.

The name of Jackie Mason would not be used for the Comedy Club I opened in Times Square. Not then. Not now. Not ever. Since I wasn't going to use Jackie Mason's name, it was back to the drawing board.

I met with the owners of "The Catch a Rising Star" brand who wanted to return to New York, but they did not want to be physically present in running the business. We agreed that it would be in the form of a licensing deal where they would license their name to my space and I would run it. Seemed like all was good. One day a " representative" of Catch (a young woman probably twenty–five years old) came in with a notebook. It was entirely filled with the action plan on how to run the club. This coming from an organization that had filed for bankruptcy twice in the last seven years for their New York locations. And they were going to teach me how to run a comedy club? No thanks.

Marty Fisher then asked if I would be interested in running an Improv in New York. I said: "What are you going to do? Make a deal with Budd Friedman?" Budd Friedman and his wife, Silver, were divorced. Budd had the rights to everything 125 miles away from the New York club and Silver got the rights to the New York Club. We would be dealing with Silver Friedman.

The "Improv" name was much more attractive to me than the "Catch a Rising Star" brand. At that time "Last Comic Standing" was a hit on national TV. A lot of the episodes were filmed at the Improv Comedy Clubs across the country. Even though the New York venue was not part of that chain, there's no doubt we would benefit from all the TV exposure. So the deal was made and my new comedy club would be opening as the Improv Comedy Club.

The opening night party for the Improv Comedy Club was spectacular. Silver Friedman invited a lot of the original club comics to come celebrate in the reopening. The party featured legendary performers Robert Klein, Richard Belzer, Joe Piscopo, Jackie Martling, Danny Aiello (who was a doorman in the original Improv), Jim Gaffigan, Freddie Roman, and Dave Attelll.

The excitement couldn't even be dampened by an agent named Roger Paul telling me that Jamie Masada (owner of the famous The Laugh Factory in Los Angeles) was opening another Laugh Factory a few blocks down from mine. Well...

it did manage to rattle me a bit. Okay. A LOT. (Within two years, however, Jamie left New York and The Laugh Factory was history.)

One comic came over to me that evening and asked if I remembered him. He seemed a bit ruffled when I didn't. "The haze of the evening," I said, "I'll be honest with you. I just don't." He said: "Ten years ago, you and I were waiting on line at The Improv on a freezing cold afternoon to audition for Silver Friedman. Then it started raining and you yelled 'Fuck this place! I'm going to own it one day.' Well, now you do."

It took almost ten years to move Uptown, but I now had the biggest name in Comedy in the biggest city in the world. The club flourished and was a hit from day one. Then Marty Fischer, my friend and a partner of Silver Friedman in this deal, pulled the pin on the grenade that would explode and nearly ruin everything.

2002 marked the 40th anniversary for the Improv Comedy Club chain. A big TV special and a 21 city tour was planned. We thought that this was going to be a chunk of fantastic publicity. However, even though we owned the name "The Improv" – the club, itself, was not part of the Improv "chain". Silver Friedman lost the rights to being part of that chain in her divorce from Budd Friedman many years before. My comedy club was not to be included in the celebration, the tour, or any of the publicity.

Now, Marty decided that without The New York Improv being included, the show couldn't go on. He decided to sue. This led to a two year lawsuit which ended in Marty Fischer and Silver Friedman completely losing their rights, and with it, me losing the rights to the name.

Everything I had was in this club, and while the last few years have been great with the name, I had no idea how it would do without it. I was terrified.

CHAPTER 11

Going it Alone:

Broadway Comedy Club

You're damned if you do and you're damned it you don't. First, I lose the biggest "name" in comedy clubs (The Improv), then I discovered that the person I licensed the name from (Silver Friedman) brutally disparaged me in the court papers. She claimed that I was a "low–brow" comedy club operator because I ran New Talent Showcases. Silver Friedman managed to lose the greatest name in comedy twice. She would've been in a dire financial state had I not licensed that name from her. Then she takes a knife and stabs me in the back by denigrating my modus operandi.

I had a rhythm. I had a business that was growing. I had stationary, a website, a lit marquee…a Brand! And right smack dab in the middle of that flow I had to disassemble, reassemble and scramble for a new name. The first thing I did was to consult with Emerson Moncure, head of our Times Square Street Team and tell him the news. Disappointed but reassuring, he told me that we can definitely move forward and move forward successfully . His positive attitude buoyed my fierce determination. Thank–you, Emerson.

I thought long and hard about it. I reached out to "Catch a Rising Star" to see if there was any interest in resuscitating that name for my club. Mr. Craig Near was the operating partner. He indicated he was willing to make a deal with the original numbers like we had talked about before it was The Improv. But it had now been twelve years since Catch was out of the New York market and a generation of people had grown up not knowing the name. To me, they're the key generation. The biggest demographic I've got. That name would be virtually meaningless to them.

"Catch a Rising Star" is a legendary name but I decided to come up with my own name. The tourists in New York? They don't give two shits about what name is on the marquee. It's a Comedy Club. It's a fun and affordable night out. That's what they care about. It was time to establish my own brand and have total control over my own destiny. It was time to grow.

After much soul–searching I came up with the name "The Broadway Comedy Club". It was 2008.

It went on to become a huge success in spite of the recession. We opened up a third showroom. Not only was I the first guy to open a comedy club with two showrooms, I became first to open two comedy clubs in one city, and the first to open one comedy club with "three" showrooms. In some corners I was labeled "The New York City King of Comedy".

My wife teases me, "You told me you were a bar owner." Through these immensely stressful times I was grateful that hard work does pay off. Grateful that I could do things my way at last. Grateful for it all.

Then a group called the Comedy Coalition was about to literally blow up a rat right at my front door.

CHAPTER 12

Ground Zero – The Family

"Comedians don't laugh. They're too busy analyzing why it's funny or not."—James Lipton, The Actor's Studio

A comic's whole world is comedy and sometimes this view is a very narrow sliver of life. Maybe that's one reason I fell in love with my wife Carolyn. She wasn't a comedian. Until I met her everybody in my sphere was comedy saturated. I needed a force outside the world of comedy that would give me a different perspective on so many issues. It was healthy and enriching to find a partner who could ground me and provide me with stability, with a sense that life is filled with other matters to both enjoy and be concerned about...and yet she's so much fun to be around. I must have done something right in this lifetime to be blessed with this true partner there for me every step of this journey who came along just when I needed her.

"David wants to wear a bra to work at the Broadway Comedy Club." Sheba Mason, a comic, told me on the phone one day. She was the catalyst in healing the emotional rift separating my son David from me before I was able to grasp and eventually totally understand his gender non-conformity. "I think he would speak to you a lot more often if you could just understand where he's coming from." Although my son David initially came out to me at the age of thirteen. I kind of suspected it all along. Suddenly a few years later David started dressing very effeminately. I couldn't seem to wrap my head around the reason why. Our interactions would be terse and tense. Although I always loved him, it was a long road to enlightenment regarding not only "acceptance" of his unique nature but awareness that is a privilege to be the parent of a Transgender child. It became an enriching adventure in my life, an adventure I now embrace.

Gender identity is not a choice, but an orientation that I believe is endowed at birth. And it isn't easy. Many times I've stared down people who have looked at my child in an awkward way. I would tell them off and then my kid would privately tell me "Dad, don't worry about it. I meet jerks like that every day." It takes courage to be who you are and I'm proud of my kid.

(Left) Dina Marie Martin; Mary Joseph (Real Housewives NJ)

Today David is "Dina" a beautiful young woman who surprises and amuses me every day.

Not that there aren't other problems commonly associated with Boomers and their Millennial kids. Ever since the age of eight Dina had been in the Comedy club scene and started helping out. I remember Chris Murphy telling someone: "You better be nice to this kid. He's going to be running the place one day." As an adult, Dina worked at The Broadway Comedy Club and I always thought she would want to take over the business. I was pleased with her work and the way she handled the affairs of business. One day at a family function she got a little tipsy and confided to me that she really doesn't like the comedy business. She'd love to go into fashion." There are times she sees how disappointed I am and claims it isn't true and that she loves comedy. In spite of everything barriers still exist but I am still hoping there will come a day when she comes to me in complete honesty on where her dreams lie.

When you are a parent of means, there's a fine line between teaching kids to be self-supportive and yet know that I'm there in case they fall. Three kids in my universe with diverse personalities but I'm proud of each of them in their own way. My daughter Melinda (the only one who has actually performed on stage) is the most passionate about comedy in the family. She has grown a lot, and has learned to deal with the people who disagree with her in a more compassionate way. I love that she's a reliable manager at Greenwich Comedy Club with a true feel for this business, and yet copes with personal adversity in life with nobility and acceptance.

And then there's Samantha. An enigma. "She's such a terrific person. So sweet. So understanding. So personable." What? My wife and I would cast a sidelong glance at each other. Were these people talking about Samantha? The surly, grumpy, nasty one who during the first years of my marriage, would bury herself in the basement in her own room we called the "dungeon"? Kids always take a parent's divorce hard. She was in the crossfire shit between my wife and her first husband.

Anyone could see that. Samantha eventually would emerge from all that to become a rational and kind adult, protective of her little sister, and respectful to her parents. Few people know that Samantha was the General Manager at Broadway comedy Club and New York Comedy Club, and the comics really took to her because she treated them fairly. She graduated college, grew tired of working every weekend at the clubs, found her niche in Event Planning, and has been extremely successful ever since. With everything it takes to run a business, maybe one day she'll come full circle.

Dina Martin, Samantha Howard, Melinda Howard
Seated: Carolyn and Al Martin

Andrew Dice Clay

Judah Friedlander

TJ Miller

Al Martin when smoking inside was legal.

Shawn Wayans

Carolyn, David Duchovny, Al, Melinda Howard

Bobby Collins and Dina Martin

Al and Carolyn in The Jackie Mason Musical

Dean McDermott, Tori Spelling's Husband

Pete Davidson

Jaye McBride Becomes the First Transgender Comic Placed in Rotation at the Manhattan Comedy Club

September 24, 2018   NiteLife Exchange   Cabaret   0

Jaye McBride was recently passed at **Broadway Comedy Club**, making her the first transgender comedian to be passed into the regular rotation of a major Manhattan comedy club. Although transgender comics perform at several New York City comedy clubs, none in Manhattan has ever invited a transgender comic to be part of their regular roster. Getting passed into a New York City club is an essential professional milestone and goal for all NYC comics.

Broadway Comedy Club owner Al Martin who had invited McBride to audition. The founders of YAAAS! Fest, NYC's biggest LGBTQ Comedy Competition, first approached Martin earlier this year, recommended McBride for an audition, which he found intriguing. Martin noted "Our crowd was comprised of fifty-percent New Yorkers and fifty- percent tourists. Both groups loved her. She killed and that's my criteria when judging comics. I ask myself 'is this comic incredibly funny?'. Jaye absolutely is. So I immediately passed her into the club."

"I'm very excited to be part of the Broadway Comedy Club lineup but also to be an example to other trans kids to show them that there is a place for us in the world," McBride said. "I'm not exactly Jackie Robinson, I mean for starters I tell more dick jokes and throw like a girl but I think it's a huge deal that this club believes in me. I can't wait to show them that they made the right call."

Al Martin With Ginger Reiter

Carolyn, Suzanne Charles (Former Miss America),Al

SNL's Jay Pharoah

Soupy Sales, Richard Pryor Jr. On Book Signing Day

The Hack Pack: Steve Marshall, Al, Chris Murphy

David Spade

Ian Wehrle, Sheba Mason, Don Rickles, Al, Carolyn

Mike Epps

Carolyn, Former Miss America Suzanne Charles,Al

CHAPTER 13

Picketing, Percolating, and Prevention

My blood was percolating. I could hear my heartbeat pounding in my ears, as I raced to the meeting with the Comedy Coalition. It was the day before they had planned to blow up a big fat rat right in the front of my establishment to make their point. My mind drifted to the days when my friend Chris Murphy had assured me how fortunate I was to be under the radar back when I opened the New York Comedy Club. I would hear the comics speaking about "real" club owners and my name had not been included, and it disturbed me. I almost wished it could be that way again. But it wasn't. I owned two Comedy Clubs and five rooms. I was a target.

Comics don't just decide to be comics and that's it: sudden stardom. Comics need to work on their act, develop new material, tweak every syllable. They need to be on stage and they need to be on stage several times a week, sometimes several times a night, for years. Some of the more lavish clubs will have a New Talent Showcase only once or twice a week, or an Open Mic very early in the day or very late at night designed to test their material before other comics. A comic will, just as I did when I started out, wait hours and hours to get on stage for five minutes.

When a person attends college, they pay tuition. Comics don't, but my five NYC Comedy rooms served the needs of a multitude of comics, from the New to the Big-name comics, I offered a plethora of opportunities. Comedy Classes. Open Mics. Bringers shows. Internships. New Talent showcases. Club shows. All the while I was providing a room and a stage I had bills to pay. Rent. Insurance. Taxes. When I became a comic in 1989, comics working in Manhattan weren't there to necessarily make a living, but were there to hone their acts enabling them to make serious money on the road. This was 2005. I guess things change.

It was at an annual Christmas party I threw at the Broadway Comedy Club when I first caught wind of the imminent furor. A certain comic who I always gave a lot of stage time to was actually walking around at the party right in front of me taking names and numbers down to start an email list to get this organization going. The purpose of the organization was to fight for higher wages in all New York City Comedy Clubs.

They particularly wanted an increase in weeknight and weekend wages, which means "all" wages. Comics in New York City were already making considerably more money than comics in Los Angeles. Comics were asking for a $15 a set increase on weekends to make up for increases and cab fare, and were also looking for a $10 increase per set on weeknights. I started to calculate all the money and realized this would cost me $25,000 to $30,000 a year, with no way to make it up. This was a real financial squeeze. I also was upset that one or two clubs were being given a pass on increases which seemed unfair to me. A couple of clubs capitulated rather quickly. I was told that of the four clubs holding out, two were mine.

I did note that only a few Big name comics were going to benefit from this – a lot of lower level comics would not. Yet these lower level comics were being recruited to work on potential picket lines. No one seemed to care much about them. It's still like that.

I was told that there had just been a meeting of all the Rank–and–File Comics. It was a very boisterous meeting. The comics were furious, and my name was being floated around as the "bad guy". Also one very unfortunate rat was shivering in his cage. He didn't care to be blown up for a publicity stunt at all. He wasn't even in comedy.

Rich Brooks was convinced us all to sit down and talk. On a Thursday afternoon I met with Russ Meneve, Ted Alexandro and Tom Schilue – the leaders of The Comedy Coalition. Fortunately there is a solution to every problem under the sun. You just have to find it. There had to be an amicable way to work this out. There was. After negotiating awhile, we reached a compromise that even the White House administration would surely praise, and a very dark day in the New York City Comedy World was averted.

And then there was Sarah.

CHAPTER 14

Ass on the Line, Heart on the Floor:

Sarah Silverman

n the early 2000s, Todd Barry, an excellent comedian, was booked for a show at New York Comedy Club. It was a packed house and the audience was the kind comics dream about. The audience was alive and sizzling. It doesn't matter how famous or popular a comic may be; it doesn't matter if he or she just stepped off the stage at Carnegie Hall, if there's money involved or not. When an audience is hot, that comic will feel compelled to jump on that stage and ride the wave of boisterous laughter. The need to be on that stage, relating to that audience, and evoking that laughter, They can't help it. That's the nature of comedians.

Sarah Silverman was a good friend of Todd Barry. That night she decided to accompany him to the club. I knew her from doing spots in various clubs and there would always be a cordial nod. I had booked Todd to perform for a specific rate at a specific time. He was on the lineup. She wasn't. But when she stepped into the room, and saw the crowd, Sarah walked over to me and asked, "Would you mind if I do a guest spot on the show?" I said, "Of course not, no problem." She was on Saturday Night Live, either writing or doing performances at the time. She was getting what we call in the business "a lot of heat." So, I said, "By all means, go up and do a guest spot."

At the end of her set, she came off stage feeling fulfilled and really happy that her new material worked. I wanted to put forward a sign of good faith. So, I offered her a $10 bill for cab fare. Sarah went outside in front of the club with Todd and Chris Murphy. They were talking in front of the club, gossiping, shooting the breeze, coming down from their sets and relaxing. All of a sudden Sarah storms back into the club, comes up to me and says, "Al, you paid Todd Barry $50? Why did you only pay me $10?" I said, "Well, first of all, Todd was booked on the show and you weren't. You were an off–the–cuff guest spot. You asked me for a spot! I didn't presume to ask you. I felt funny not paying you anything at all, so out of appreciation, I gave you some car fare. But in all honesty, you weren't booked for a spot, you had an unplanned Guest Spot."

She wasn't satisfied. "Well, I still think I should have gotten the same as him." I retorted, "Well, you probably shouldn't have gotten anything at all. It was a Guest Spot." She left visibly angry.

Generally, when a noteworthy comedian does a guest spot, you don't need to pay them. In some circles, it can even be insulting to offer someone with substantial fame and notoriety money for a drop in. It was just a guest spot, but I wanted to show her some token of appreciation. I was hoping she would feel encouraged to drop by again and do additional spots.

I sincerely thought I was being nice. She didn't.

Through the years, I would hear from various people that whenever my name would come up in a conversation with Sarah, she'd pipe up that I wronged her.

More than ten years later, in 2014, I was vacationing with my family in Florida. Expecting a few weeks of peace, relaxation, and quiet, my phone blows up. Message after message comes in: "Did you read the news about you?" "It's in Salon. It's on NBC. It's in Newsday!" Now a household name, Sarah Silverman was accusing me of sexism. The Daily News reposted Silverman's accusation, and it was getting traction on social media.

Gender–Gap wage inequality is a topic that infuriates people and is a big issue in national politics. It's a topic that I feel very strongly about. I have three daughters and I would never want to see them make any less money than a man for the same work. My wife was a New York City school teacher and I would have been infuriated if she was making less money than any man for the same job. I've been in comedy over twenty years and if I was consistently paying women less than men on any gender basis, I wouldn't have had nearly the success or respect from the comics I did.

One female comic came to my defense on The Conan O'Brien show. "You could say a lot of things about Al Martin. You could call Al Martin cheap. You could call Al Martin stingy, but he's stingy to everyone. He's just as stingy to male comedians as he is to female comedians."

I made a selfie video, posted it on my Facebook page, on Broadway Comedy Club's page, on Greenwich Village Comedy Club's page and all across social media. The little video went viral with over 250,000 views. I got hundreds of responses – shockingly in support! I was getting calls from both right and left leaning websites and publications. I was on NBC, CBS, and ABC. It became a kind of war on

Silverman because of her outspoken political beliefs and publicity wise, Sarah was taking a pummeling. Salon was a left-leaning publication that gave Sarah hero status, but my side of the story was gaining traction, too. And to boot, many female comedians came to my defense. Their quasi-flattering response would often be: "Al Martin is cheap to everyone equally."

I certainly didn't mind. I have no problem with being called stingy or cheap. It's part of my tough, self-starter, struggling-to-make-something-of-myself kind of way. I had to start from scratch, hustling, putting two dimes together. I started my clubs on a shoe-string. Even though I had a reputation of being a hard businessman and someone who watched every penny and how it was spent, people saw I wasn't doing it in an evil or abusive way. I paid everybody, yeah, maybe poorly through the years, but not that much crappier than other clubs. And everyone was paid the same crap. Equal crap. Not Gender-Gap crap! Not here.

Good Morning America interviewed me to run the story. The very next morning Sarah Silverman issued a public apology saying she was sorry. She did not mean to say anything derogatory about me and knew Al Martin for many years. "He was a very nice man who always treated me fairly," she said. "I would go into New York Comedy Club and do my sets in Al's club and I always signed the Book." (The book was where comedians signed for their pay.) Funny thing is, in 2000, I didn't have a Pay Book. But I'm happy as hell that she signed it!

In the comedy business, not too many suns rise and set before another crisis occurs; another well-intended good deed turns sour; another situation where my ass is on the line and my heart is on the floor.

In the summer of 2007 I started receiving phone calls from people cursing me out. They were calling me a terrorist, a terrorist supporter and an anti-Israel Zealot. Me? A guy who loves Jackie Mason, bagels and lox, and anything with a 'shmear' on it? A guy who has always been a proud Jew? I'm a terrorist? Nothing could be more absurd.

Debbie Schlussel, a frequent Fox News contributor and popular online blogger, claimed I had written a letter to Judge Joan Azrack praising a person who had threatened her life. Ms. Schlussel wrote on her blog:

"Judge Azrack sentenced Mr. John to only 4 months in prison (plus 400 hours of community service), even though she was actually required to sentence him to 12–18 months, as required by the sentencing guidelines. In addition, Federal Probation Officer Jeffrey Houser recommended that Mr. John receive a year in prison, the maximum sentence for the misdemeanor, to which soft Justice Department officials allowed him to plea in a very generous deal. It is rare that a Federal Judge does not follow the recommendation of the Probation Officer, even rarer that she goes so much softer on the criminal."

Schlussel continued that, "Among the letters Mr. John submitted to the court for leniency was one by New York Comedy Club owner Al Martin." She called for a boycott of The New York Comedy Club.

WHAT THE FUCK?

Years earlier, Robert John took one of my comedy classes. Back then he asked me for a Letter of Recommendation. I get requests for Letters of Recommendation from comics all the time for jobs or apartments. To me he was just another kid from the Bronx trying to become a Comedian. I wrote something to the effect that "He took my class and was a good student and took the work seriously." I had no idea that his middle name was Mustaq; that later on in life he would morph into a Jihadi; or that he would take my letter and misrepresent it in court. I especially didn't know that he was going to threaten to behead Ms. Schlussel (a joke, he later claimed). She had to wait four years for her case to go to court. It took three minutes before my phone started ringing off the hook.

I wrote an email to Ms. Schlussel and explained that I had no idea how he would twist my words around – especially for such a horrific reason. Fortunately, she updated her blog:

"Mr. Martin contacted me, telling me he was duped into writing the letter, that he was never aware what was involved. I feel bad for him given what he has written me, so I withdraw my call for you to boycott his New York Comedy Club. But I must say that he was very easily duped because he failed to investigate why he was writing the letter."

The next person who asked me for a Letter of Recommendation would be in big trouble.

CHAPTER 15

MY Book – MY Gripes:
Jim Gaffigan and Lisa Lampanelli

Jim Gaffigan was never my favorite comic. When The New York Comedy Club was on 48th Street in the early '90s he was new and not remotely edgy. That didn't stop him from insisting that I put him on a line–up with Bill Hicks, Lizz Winstead, and Dave Attell. He wanted to advance. I get it. But I couldn't put him in the main line–up. It was my club and my choice. Jim always held a grudge about it.

One night at the Comedy Cellar, one of my managers, Brad Trackman, was in the audience. Jim totally went off on him, blaming him, and then peppering his act with a series of brutal insults against me. Poor Brad had to endure this vicious onslaught. Years later, when I opened the Improv Comedy Club (now The Broadway Comedy Club) in Manhattan, Jim Gaffigan would be there every day. Jim was friends with my manager and comedy booker Rich Brooks. He would be there seven nights a week. It's a unique club because tourists flock to it. It's always packed and it's a favorite venue for comedians to work out before a national tour or TV spot. Rich was his opening act on the road and he would double as Jim's sound man and road manager.

One evening at The Borgata in Atlantic City, my wife and I were enjoying Rich's opening set. Jim went up next with his typical whining routines and I found it bizarre. Even though he was headlining in Atlantic City, I couldn't get into his style. In the middle of his set, in a thousand seat venue, I picked myself up and walked out hoping that someone, anyone notice or even care. They didn't. Jim went on to create a TV Land series based on his married life called The Jim Gaffigan Show, had several successful TV comedy specials, and published two books. I never saw him again and I never looked back.

Lisa Lampanelli was a different story. I loved her style immediately. I was performing at The Joker's Comedy Club in Westchester County, Connecticut in the early years of The New York Comedy Club. When she stepped on stage, the audience found her absolutely hysterical, very raw and very funny. She had been a reputed marketer and was actively networking as a member of the Friars Club. She was a real people person and a great conversationalist.

Lisa also had a side hustle booking New Talent shows at Caroline's Comedy Club (one of the most famous Comedy Clubs in the country). Lisa was booking a lot of those shows and probably making a lot of money. She rose up the ranks of The Friar's Club to became head of their admissions committee. She was ultimately asked to do the Friar's Roasts, and here she developed her own style, a sharp-witted insult type routine, along the lines of Don Rickles, only much filthier.

Lisa invited me one night to participate in a panel discussion. Young comedians would ask questions of comedy club owners. The Friars Club sponsored this event in order to meet club owners and see how they might make improvements in their own club. I enthusiastically accepted and afterward received a huge thank you, a big hug, was told how absolutely wonderful I was. Lisa thanked me profusely for participating.

A few months earlier I had been approached to join the Friar's Club. My application was going fine until one day, after the panel, my sponsor called with bad news. There was an objection to my membership. The head of the application committee – Lisa Lampanelli – was leading a charge against me because my club had New Talent Showcases. I was the guy who invented New Talent Showcases years ago! She stole the idea from me! Now she was using it against me?

'Seinfeld' gave us the term: "World Collision" when two separate aspects in a person's life collide. Lampanelli was guilty of World Collision. I should have been welcomed as a member of The Friars Club. She let healthy competition get in the way. Above all, she should have never shaken my hand, hug me and sweetly pretend to welcome me.

There's not a profession in the world which doesn't manifest its own unique set of gripes. Teachers, Doctors, Scientists. Everybody's got 'em. That's what this dimension on earth is partially about – dealing with gripes and moving on. Comedy is no different. I am the receiver of gripes of all kinds. From comedy club bookers, managers, patrons, employees, family, friends, neighbors, the government, and of course comedians. But since this is my book, it's my turn to air my gripes. I mentioned these two comics not only because they're celebrities, but they represent two of my most major gripes. Jim and Lisa, however, are not the only ones. I could randomly choose any two lesser known comics, and chances are, some will irk me in exactly the same way. This has happened too often in my career. The spirit of competition in the Comedy World dons a false veil which emboldens phoniness. And that HURTS.

CHAPTER 16

An Olive Branch or Blood:
Greenwich Comedy Club

I will never condone Socialism. I love the idea of an individual with dreams having the freedom to try, to win, to lose, and to pick himself up and try again. I embrace Capitalism in this great country with every fiber of my being and the healthy competition that accompanies it. Competition is inspiring. Barking is the foundation of Capitalism. Going as far back to the ancient bazaars, salesmen have been loudly hawking their wares, pitching their products to the innocent passerby who hopefully gets drawn in. It is no different with Barkers selling comedy tickets on every street corner in New York City. Sometimes, however, a novice will violate the rules, and in an unsanctioned act, he will try to get someone standing on a line at The Comedy Cellar to go to your show. The owner will come out justifiably fuming and castigate the knucklehead. The feud then spills over to the people you care about. Welcome to the opening of the Greenwich Village Comedy Club.

Once The Broadway Comedy Club opened with its three rooms operating full steam, the Street Team prioritized Broadway's sales over New York Comedy Club's since Broadway was closer to their Times Square operation. People could just trot. Right on over and enjoy themselves. By 2011, The New York Comedy Club began treading water. It didn't help that I had been there twenty–four years and during that entire time, there was that sole resident on the block dialing 311 with daily noise complaints.

I grew weary with The New York Comedy Club and I always loved the vibe and energy of Greenwich Village.

A Real estate broker contacted me about an available Greenwich Village space. The landlord was having a lot of problems with its current tenant, a music venue, creating too much noise. Apparently music is louder than comedy. The bass boomed constantly. The drums rattle the neighbors' nerves. Through the walls. Through their very veins. One neighbor (a writer) needed absolute silence to focus. (Why a writer would rent an apartment on the "Bourbon Street"of New York is beyond me.) Nevertheless, those bass sounds bombarding the neighbors made an ideal opening for me. The Landlords of MacDougal Street needed a replacement business venue. This section of the street was lined with stores which hawking T–shirts, handbags, and bellydancing scarves. They needed an entertainment component working in tandem with those shops. Something with less noise than those electric guitars wailing and drums pounding out the beat. Music is louder than comedy. The Greenwich Village Comedy Club was born.

The intimate space which was perfect for a sixty seat old school comedy club. This area of New York City has a very tough process to get a liquor license:

Step #1: Appear in front of a liquor license committee.

Step #2: If the committee approves it, take your case to the Community Board.

Step #3: Convince The Bleecker Area Merchants and Residents Association (BAMRA) a combination of a block association and business improvement district.

The Community Board asked me to present my case in a specific way to "BAMRA". Their main concerns were noise pollution and street congestion. They asked me to make a presentation and to explicitly state how my business would not interfere with or add to the normal congestion of The Comedy Cellar just down the street – I had no desire to even broach the subject of The Comedy Cellar, a highly reputed, respected, and popular club. I had I was told that I would have to mention them in order to get the needed approval.

Following the board's instructions, I stood and explained how we would rotate our show times so not to be in conflict with The Comedy Cellar or add to the street congestion. Noam Dworman, the owner of The Comedy Cellar, was in the audience. Undoubtedly having his own issues with the community board, he was extremely displeased that I mentioned The Comedy Cellar in any capacity. His fury begat a turf that defied logic. Working at The Comedy Cellar is a dream of many comedians. Dustin Chafin was "passed" there and had been performing periodically.

Comedians are free agents who stand on stage and tell jokes. They care only about the laughter. And when they take giant steps up the ladder of success, they are then told they can't work "everywhere". This is not because of their talent, but because they stand on a stage in some other club a block down the street. Or in a nearby town.

I had a long conversation with Dustin early on, pointing out that managing the Greenwich Village Comedy Club would probably jeopardize his ability to work at The Comedy Cellar.

Within a few days, Noam called Dustin in and told him that he could continue performing at The Cellar only if he was not involved in my new club. But Dustin was steadfast and stuck with me. Dustin made a hard choice that day, giving up a sure thing for a bet on the underdog. His loyalty is exceptional. He's been with us ever since.

In the next few years the Comedy Cellar would initiate multiple rules on MacDougal Street in the spirit of fierce competition. I was once a guest on the Comedy Cellar Podcast, and I pointed out to Noam that I am the person who spurred him on to expand his comedy empire. In his quest to compete, he opened multiple rooms in the area. That is the glory of Capitalism and I wish him luck.

CHAPTER 17

The Pariah and The Charmer –

The End of an Era

"Maybe you guys should just buy the club." I said. I was kidding. All of a sudden they looked at me and asked "How much?" I was shooting the shit with Emilio Savone and Scott Lindner, a street team that I hired two years before to help pull up the numbers at The New York Comedy Club.

I was taken aback. I might've bitched and moaned about the club a lot, but I never seriously considered what it would be worth to sell. It had been part of my world for twenty–four years. I couldn't imagine life without it... could I?

Greenwich Village Comedy Club opened two years earlier. It sucked up a lot of my cash flow. It's not in my nature to accrue debt, but oh – the debt – it was accruing. Both my sister and my mom had taken ill and I had been contributing heavily to them financially; added to that was the closing of both clubs for a few weeks in 2012 due to Hurricane Sandy, and needing some uninsured repairs on my home in Staten Island. I was for the first time in many years in a real financial squeeze. Times were tough.

Our Broadway Comedy Club Street Team went through a change in management and became extremely weak. The amount of people they were bringing in decreased by seventy percent. I hired an old school street team from the Comic Strip to energize sales. Emilio and Scott were classic, but the Broadway team clashed with these guys in Times Square. It was bad, and it just wasn't working any longer. I asked Emilio and Scott to focus on The New York Comedy Club. That helped. A little.

An increase in expenses and a decrease in revenue is never a good thing. OK. I'll admit it. I wasn't in a mere financial squeeze. I was bleeding. Then these two guys, with their passion, enthusiasm, energy and youth, said: "How much?"

I stepped outside the club and glanced across the street. Was it really one misanthrope who complained constantly that managed to get this little place investigated by the Building Department, The Fire Department, The Health Department, The Department of Environmental Preservation and the New York City Police Department? Or did they all just hate me? They had been gnawing and gnawing at me. Any one of these inspections could morph into something that can cost you your liquor license. I'm just one man trying to eke out a decent living and fill the world with laughter. If you lose your liquor license in a single location, you can lose it at all your businesses. Isn't life supposed to be fun and easy at times? This little club was hardly making a profit now. The risk to the other two clubs was not worth it. And I was so wrapped up in the burdensome neighbors that I couldn't give Greenwich my all.

I knew what I had to do. Selling the New York Comedy Club would eradicate all my debt. I would keep Broadway and Greenwich and sell The New York Comedy Club to Emilio and Scott. I stepped inside and saw the hope and determination on their faces. I knew I was doing the right thing.

"You two may just be able to resuscitate The New York Comedy Club." I could feel it. Nothing would stop them from their dream. "Let's make it work, but first we have to deal with the shit that goes with it."

In order for the sale to go through I needed permission from the landlord, the new buyers must get approved by the Community Board and subsequently the State Liquor Authority. The Danny DeVito clone sold the building years before and the new owner easily facilitated a lease for them.

The block despised me and they did not want another comedy club to come after my reign. They wanted everything about this comedy club to vanish from their lives. The Community Board was not easy at all. The talk was to reject the new owners' application.

The process in New York State is that every two years your Liquor License is up for renewal. If the Community Board has any complaints they have to make them right away. The State Liquor Authority then contemplates what they want to do, Every two years for the last ten renewals the Community Board voted to deny me my license, but as I had no violations of any sort including underage drinking, or riots or problems at the location, The State Liquor Authority saw no reason to agree with them. Despite The Community Board recommending again in 2014 to deny my license, the State Liquor Authority renewed me.

Emilio, a sharp-looking guy, stood sincerely and humbly before the Community Board and told them that they had a choice: They could deal with the likes of Al Martin for eternity or take a shot with us. We will do everything possible to please you and we can do a lot better. The Community Board was charmed. They were in.

In July 2014 we closed on the sale of the New York Comedy Club to the new owners. The night before the closing we had our low–key goodbye party. I wanted an intimate group of good friends to be there – those who had been instrumental in my life from day one in comedy. We ate, we laughed and we drank. We toasted a great twenty–four year run. The new owners had their own ideas and their own vibrant energy. Many of the comics that were in the room that night, young and old, knew that they were no longer going to partake in that special something they had known all their professional careers. That part was over. We toasted The New York Comedy Club one last time. I raised my kids, and grew as a person in many ways in that little place. I locked the door one last time and said good night to an unforgettable chapter of my life.

As for the new owners, I couldn't ask for better people to continue the legacy of NYCC, themselves starting out as the Underdog and fulfilling their own unique vision. Each year the owners of various comedy clubs are invited to do The Comedy Cellar Podcast in an episode titled "The Owners Round Table". I remember having a chat with Emilio and Scott, and telling them that I would be on that podcast. They looked hurt. They couldn't understand why they, as owners of a comedy club in Manhattan, had not been invited. I quoted the words of my friend Chris Murphy: "Enjoy being under the radar as long as you can."

They looked at me puzzled.

And Another Thing...

"Life's not about how hard of a hit you can give. It's about how many you can take, and still keep moving forward." —Rocky Balboa

'll admit it. I don't know everything when it comes to talent. Comics look to me with their pleading eyes for approval, but what the fuck do I really know? Give me a steak. I can tell you if it's quality, if it's succulent. But there's a very long list of comics I refused to place in the main lineup who went on to stardom. Melissa Rauch, for one. When my friend Chris Murphy suggested Melissa, I told her she wasn't ready for the lineup. Meanwhile she went on to play Bernadette in the mega-hit Big Bang Theory. There have been so many that I overlooked in the talent department that if I had any kind of conscience at all, I would find it very disturbing. Fortunately, I don't.

Sure. I have my favorites: Greg Geraldo, who started at The New York Comedy Club open-mic which he was kind enough to mention in his book: "A Comedian's Story". However, he passed away young and deprived the world of his talent. He is sorely missed.

Guess I have to lump the following group in my top tier of favorites; Rodney, Jackie Mason, Kevin James (because he's fat), Joan Rivers and Don Rickles, (three of whom are dead, and one of whom tells everyone to "drop dead on Tuesday" while sticking his fork in their lunch and the other whom would be amazing playing me in the movie version of this book).

Then there's Marc Maron, an edgy comic who doesn't sugar-coat but tells it like it is, and has had numerous TV appearances. There is something about him I always loved watching and he now has a very successful WTF PODCAST. Gregg Rogell was strong from day one, always growing and working hard, and Corey Kahaney has gone on to big success; she still makes me laugh on and off stage. The "nicest guy in the club" label goes to the very talented DC Benny.

On the polar opposite end of the scale is a certain phony no-talent jerk who spent his time nagging, nagging, nagging, wanting stage time and thought he was better than he was. Still – I gave him stage-time. Think about it. The rent. The equipment. The liquor. The food. I pay for all of it so some back-stabbing conceited amateur can jump on my stage and learn his craft, only to have him turn against me in a furor of demands. One day standing in front of the Boston Comedy Club, this vile human being walks up to me and shouts: "Hey Al! How are you? How is it going?" All friendly-like. Three days later I find out he was calling for my head in a mass meeting of comics organized to form the Comedy Coalition. Chances are you never heard of him and you certainly won't hear of him here in this paragraph on this page. His initials are D.D.

Sometimes comedy club owners are fucked–over. It's true. We are not immune to hurt, and disloyal comics can kick us hard. We give them a start and there is an unspoken agreement that should he or she make it bigger somehow, they will thank you or mention you and somehow shine the light on the club where they took their first baby–steps. That rarely happens. The comic, however, who stands out the most and hurt my partner, is Rich Vos.

Don Siegel gave Rich a great deal of work. In Manhattan, Dangerfields and I were the first to book him. Rich got his big break on Last Comic Standing. We were truly excited and anticipated that the now super–hot Rich Vos would work the club at least occasionally. It would have been a major break since the competing chain was choking us from getting big names. Lo and behold, Rich would not work for us at all. He would not even stop by. He would not drop in to work on new material. No way in hell. He was afraid to jeopardize his relationship with the big chain clubs. I never forgot his disloyalty to Don Siegel who provided him with a lot of paydays when he was a total unknown. A few years later, when the "heat" wore off, Rich was willing to work for us. I told my partner if we could get him for the right price, it would be fine. We should let negative feelings from the past evaporate. Don wanted nothing to do with him ever again. His resentment and hurt were palpable. It was the one time I didn't argue with him.

And there are others. So many others who conveniently forget who gave them a start. Either they think it doesn't bother us or they just don't give a shit. Take Mike Bochetti. I love Mike Bochetti. He is the quintessential underdog. Mike would travel three hours one way just to get a spot. He is endowed with an incredible work ethic and fierce determination. One day I receive a tape from a nut with disjointed thoughts and crazy jokes. It was so bizarre that I mentioned it to a bunch of my friends. A few days later Mike shows up at the mic and introduces himself, asking me if I remembered his tape. He was an instant hit. Even comics who had grown weary of watching other comics all seemed to want to watch Mike. (A truly rare breed of comic like a Rich Shapiro or the ventriloquist Otto and George can inspire other comics.) This comic with his innocent mannerisms and ticks made him lovable. Mike must have told me a million times: "When I make it, I'm going to let the world know I started with you, Al!" One day, he tipped me off to watch the Howard Stern show, assuring me that New York Comedy Club would get a mention. My wife, Carolyn, and I were excited. Finally someone would remember to thank us publicly.

It was a special night. We sat glued to the TV screen with a giant bowl of hot popcorn, and some wine. Stern specifically asks Mike which club he wants to plug. He blurts out: "Eastville Comedy Club!" Apparently Eastville promised him a spot for a plug. There was fire flaring out of my wife's nostrils, as she threw the popcorn at the screen. Mike has gone on to much success. He was a finalist in Last Comic

Standing and appeared on Opie and Anthony. He appears with Louis CK and Judah Friedlander on projects and is working as a co-host on Artie Lange's radio show and Podcast. He, however, had better not run into my unforgiving wife.

Disheartening failures and disappointments don't stop there. Not by any means.

Bababooey. He is best known as Gary Dellabate, Howard Stern's long time producer. Whatever Howard might say about him, if you don't go through Gary, you never speak to Howard. He was that trusted. Back in the early 90's, I was looking for ways to put New York Comedy Club on the map. So I booked Gary (AKA Boy Gary) for a personal appearance for $800 and in exchange he had agreed to plug his appearance on the Stern show. Weeks. Days. Hours passed until his appearance. I never heard a single mention, acknowledgment, or plug. Three people showed up for Gary's show. Three people in the room. Gary requested his

$800. I paid him $200 just to leave the club so I could control the urge to punch the shit out of him.

For all the coal I am handed, however, I every so often find a diamond beneath. Since then many Howard Stern alumni have appeared at my venues...Jackie Martling, Sal the Stockbroker, Richard Christy, Benjy Bronk and Shuli Egar. But it was the comics who did not rely only on the Stern show, like Shuli and Martling who became solid comics in their own right.

Road Comics and City Comics. Two entirely different genres of comedians. One travels for hours for shit money, and the other stays in the city and works for shittier money. The City Comics regard the Road Comics with disdain. Working on the road away from your peers fosters bad habits like stealing material and doing what is known as Hack material. Often road comics sadly toil their entire career away in relative obscurity. City Comics hope to get that break in front of TV scouts or hope to be seen by potential managers. Some go on to manage other comedians like Jeff Sussman who represents Kevin James. Others successfully straddled both worlds like Jammin Jim Florentine, a Rock and Roll comic who I consider one of those diamonds who sparkled beneath the fray. Jim booked a lot of rooms and always provided me with work. Jim Norton, another funny motherfucker from New Jersey who I was fortunate to work with numerous times, has had incredible radio success. These guys engender a sense of gratitude in me just by having known them.

The brush–off. The big rebuff. The slap across the face. All due to no fault of your own. I got plenty of that as well. Scott Krantz, the talent coordinator of The Toyota Comedy Festival 1990s was expecting an extra–special show from us and unlike most other clubs who kept the allotted $500 and did nothing special at all, I wanted to do a Sitcom Star–Studded type of show. Something different, even if it meant digging into my own pocket. Local agent Roger Paul booked the comics. That night, two of the bigger names did not show. Scott Krantz, (who was also the booker for Stand Up

New York Comedy Club) was infuriated. At me. Even though I had nothing to do with the two comics who didn't show up. If had known their whereabouts I would have dragged them from the bowels of the earth and slammed them onto the stage where they had committed to be. Krantz banned my club from future participation in the Toyota Comedy Festival.

Maybe that's when I learned that a permanent "ban" is soul-crushing. Maybe that's why when people do me wrong, I "ban" them, but in most cases, it is not permanent. I grab whatever sliver of forgiveness I can find and throw them a rope. Because I know what it feels like.

I've been told that this quality I have is extremely compassionate and even rabbinical, and could be the reason that good things come my way as well. The following year I was able to secure sponsorship from "Major Chevrolet" a huge Queens, New York, car dealership. They gave me $2500 which is five times the budget I was getting from Toyota, and thus the Major Chevrolet Comedy Festival was born. Shortly thereafter, Scott Krantz was no longer working at Stand Up New York and the Toyota Comedy Festival evaporated into the night. I'd like to conclude this matter by adding: Go fuck yourself Scott Krantz but please know that I forgive you!

And the deals! The deals that I had with this one and that one, that would all collapse. The hope. The paperwork. The of hours time and energy put in to each deal, only to see them kicked to the curb. Like the time Cary Hoffman (a successful talent manager and an incredible Frank Sinatra impersonator) who also owned Stand Up New York Comedy Club, spread the word that he wanted out of the club. I feverishly worked on the deal. I really wanted to own that club. And I walked up five flights of stairs to meet with the landlord of the place several times. That's not an easy thing to do when you're a big guy who loves to eat as much as I do. To me it was like climbing Mount Kilimanjaro. Hoffman was eager to close the sale, but there was a caveat: I wanted the deal closed in June. He wanted to close it in September. He wanted to deprive me of a thriving, vibrant summer of sales. The usual handshake at the end of a deal morphed into a mutual middle finger gesture and a loud and resounding Fuck You! There's an old saying that the deal you don't make is sometimes the best deal. The Great Recession occurred shortly thereafter. Other doors were destined to open. And Frank Sinatra impersonators are going the way of the rotary phone, but for now, I think I'll sit back, smoke a cigar, and listen to my favorite Sinatra song: "My Way".

THANK–YOU!

Gushing with Gratitude

"I was standing in Al Martin's New York Comedy Club, and a guy comes over to me and says: 'Excuse me sir. Do you know where the toilet is?' I said: 'You're in it.'" —MORTY STORM"

In closing I would like to thank a few people:

Morty Storm is NOT one of those people (and I say that lovingly). RIP Morty. I hope it's a lot classier where you are now.

All the guys who booked me when I had nothing to offer except a couple of hundred extra pounds, who used me not for my talent, but just because I happened to show up with a car: Bob Levy, Jim Florentine, Dennis Ross (RIP) , Rick Morgan, Phil Selman , Dave Labarca, and Roger Paul.

Bob Golub. An actor in the movie "Goodfellas"(1990) is given a scene with specific dialogue: "Two people stole my truck." Five simple words. Bob Golub instead, decided to yell: "Two N!&#&#s stole my truck!". Today it would be considered racist, which is his pet peeve. Why is it okay for the whole world to still make fun of my Polish nationality? A Mexican walked up to me and said 'You Polish? You stupid?" Bob gave me the key which opened the door to Atlantic City, Vegas, Hollywood and TV. Sure, he shot a load into my toupee that one night long ago, but that single act liberated me from the Hair Club for Men. I also wish herein to apologize to his wife Emily from LA who served us a mean Shrimp Jumbalaya and afterward I advised him to marry her. Sorry Emily.

Ross Mark. Thank—you for ensuring that I was scared as shit when Steve Schirripa (the terrifying, imposing presence Bobby Baklava in The Sopranos) welcomed me to The

Riviera Hotel in Vegas to do twenty-one shows with my name up in lights at The Improv Comedy Club. Ross – You gave me a TV credit by inserting me into one of the last episodes of "An Evening at The Improv". And for that I am eternally grateful. Most comics can do a lot with a TV credit. I did nothing with it actually.

Eric Hanson. Sometimes you see a bunch of people graduating from a comedy class, doing their thing on stage and you ask yourself, who will succeed, who will fail, and who will be become your solid rock of a comedy club manager a decade later. Well, that guy is Eric Hanson. He is like the Captain of the ship guiding me through turbulence, through conflict, through the occasional stuffed-up toilet with the utmost professionalism. Hiring Eric is one of the best moves I ever made. Ending this paragraph now is an even better one.

Rich Brooks. Navigating nightly through the perilous waters of dozens of comics wanting stage time requires skilled management. Puncture an ego here. Deflate an ego there.

Unwittingly crushing a comic's spirit and deciding who will get on stage tonight and who won't, is not an easy task especially if you have a heart. Fortunately Rich Brooks doesn't. Rich claims that the slate is even; that I helped him through a tough time in his life when I asked him to manage the club. Yet it was he who brought Jim Gaffigan back to the Broadway Comedy Club which facilitated its great reputation in the early 2000s; it is he who brought me to the table with The Comedy Coalition and facilitated a peace plan; it is he whose advice I seek on so many matters. It is he who will not ask for a raise next year I hope.

Steve Arons. In 1990 there were so many young comics doing open–mics who were destined to make it big: Judah Friedlander, Sarah Silverman, Dave Attelll. Some weren't – like Steve Arons, but that's where I met him and eventually hired him to do some managing shifts at The New York Comedy Club. I was having dinner once a few blocks away when he called me and I realized he fucked up something so big that I ran over to the club to fire him. Then I asked him if he would please remember to lock up for the night. Because when you hire and fire someone so often you can't remember from minute to minute what the current status is. There is a plethora of reasons why I love this Drama Queen. He had a theatrical way about him that belied his toughness. He grew up in an era when being gay was not commonly acceptable and growing up in the closet is not easy. It's Pioneers like Steve, who paved the way for children like mine. Thank–you for that, Steve! (Steve has never said no to me for anything. That's undoubtedly because he never had a life).

The Hack Pack

Mike King: What's a Pediatric Dentist doing in the comedy world? Mike King came along in the first year or two at The New York Comedy Club. A very funny guy with a low–key delivery. "If you can throw me a paid spot, that would be great since I haven't had one since my Bar Mitzvah " he told me. In the early days my clubs were work–out rooms. I wasn't able to pay the comics much. By day he was a dentist, by night he was a comic who stood–out on stage and has had a couple of national TV appearances. It is reported that presently he does a one–man show about being a Pediatric Dentist–turned–Comic, in Chinese restaurants for groups of three or four, which everyone is happy to attend since he pays for their meal.

Chris Murphy. "A girl sitting at a bar doesn't tell you that she has a boyfriend until the moment she takes a sip of the drink you just bought her. Then it's 'My boyfriend does this. My boyfriend does that.'" A real funny joke, part of Chris Murphy's act. In reality, he is a generous guy in many ways. He never minded paying for drinks or doling out good advice. He was a caring guy, when I was first starting out, in–between, and now. I can't even fathom what the road would have been like without his special kindness. I should really be treating this Golden friend much better than I do, but rest assured, it's never going to happen. That's the kind of guy I am.

Steve Marshall: "I grew up so poor that I appreciate everything that I don't have now." This comic is probably one of the funniest guys in the business. "My father was so bad, he got a DUI on his driving test and that was only the written part." Steve is another Brooklyn underdog like me. He's crude and rude and raw.

He was working for the people who were trying to blackball acts from working for me, but he stood steadfastly in my corner even though it cost him money. I don't know just how much money it cost him, but I'm pretty sure from the looks of his clothing, he needed every penny.

For thirty years straight, our Hack Pack (King, Murphy, and Marshall) meets two or three times each year at a deli or cafe, and that is it. Nothing more. But we leave voicemail messages chronicling our current frustrations and funny experiences much more often, while being sure never to answer the phone because we really do not want to talk to each other if there's no sandwich involved.

Sheba Mason. I hereby apologize if Sheba Mason was your server when you came to the New York Comedy Club in 2004 and your drink ended up on your lap. After one too many trays of drinks crashing to the floor, it was determined that the world be safer if Sheba Mason was up on the stage instead of on the floor. She came to me, a nineteen–year–old kid, and like my own children, sometimes drove me insane, but evolved into a successful young woman and a tremendous comedian. Can't be easy when your father is a comedy legend and doesn't do one fucking thing to help you and then one day makes a play for you because he doesn't recognize you. Most young people would go to therapy for their rest of their lives if other comics constantly came up to them and flaunted how much Sheba's father had helped them. Not Sheba. She confronts it head–on. "You really wanted my father, but since you couldn't afford him, you got me," she tells certain audiences at corporate gigs.

My Three Kids. Each one of you pulled me out of that certain "shell" which insulates self–absorbed single guys, and taught me what it is to experience empathy. Were it not for you, there would have been a lot less love in my life and I could have truly enjoyed myself. Instead I learned what it is to consider other peoples' feelings first. You all helped me to become a better person, and to appreciate Social Distancing before it became mandatory – like living in Florida while you are New York.

Carolyn, My Wife. I never could have done any of it without you. You not only wear my rock – you are my rock. We made a promise to each other to live life and "Never let go. No matter what. Never let go." You kept your promise to me. I hope I kept it to you. I also want to thank you from the bottom of my heart for getting plastic surgery and an O-ring.

Those who have passed and who have worked for me off and on, and at this point are probably wondering why: Ozzie Baez (RIP) and Linda Corke (RIP).

Those who work for me currently and wonder why each day: Ernie Mack, Walter Frasier, Jason Ellis, Dan Tamayo,

Alejandro Ramos. The waitstaff. The people whose asses that were frozen cold in Times Square selling tickets. Thank–you all.

Lenny Schuss (RIP). Even comedy club owners had childhoods. He was my good friend and I miss him.

Mommy and my Sister: I have one of each. I also have a brother. (Sister has since passed away from COVID19, April 2020.)

To all the Comics who have graced and continue to grace my stages. All you ever want to do is bring people the joy of laughter. It's a noble deed I assure you. The bible says: "A merry heart is good for the soul." As I sit here ensconced in a world commandeered by a tiny little virus, I look very forward to the day, when all you comics are up there doing your sets, with the customers laughing loudly, and the cash registers ringing humming.

Lastly, Ginger Reiter. Thanks for taking all of my disjointed sentences and scattered thoughts to help me write this book and try to make it amusing.